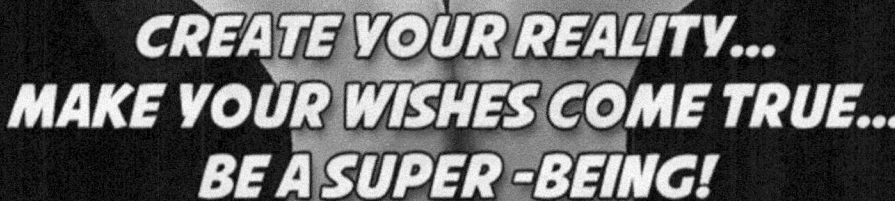

# BECOME A SUPER-BEING
## Easy Spells For Money, Luck and Love
By Dragonstar

**Global Communications/Inner Light Publications**

# Become A Super-Being
## Easy Spells For Money, Luck and Love

By Dragonstar

Copyright © 2013- Global Communications/Inner Light Publications
All Rights Reserved

Printed in the United States of America

No part of this book may be reproduced, stored in retrieval system or transmitted in any form by any means, electronic, mechanical, photocopying, recording or otherwise without the express permission of the publisher. Please address any questions about this book to: mrufo8@hotmail.com

Timothy Green Beckley: Editorial Director
Carol Ann Rodriguez: Publishers Assistant
Tim R. Swartz: Editor
Sean Casteel: Associate Editor
William Kern: Associate Editor
Cover Graphics: Tim R. Swartz

For Free Subscription To The Conspiracy Journal Write:
Tim Beckley/Global Communications
Box 753, New Brunswick, NJ 08903

Email: mrufo8@hotmail.com

www.ConspiracyJournal.Com
www.TeslasSecretLab.Com

# Contents

Introduction ............................................................................................................. 6

CHAPTER ONE – WHAT IS ALCHEMY? ............................................................ 9

CHAPTER TWO – THE NATURE OF REALITY ................................................. 22

CHAPTER THREE – THE POWER OF THE MIND ............................................. 34

CHAPTER FOUR – EVERYTHING OLD IS NEW AGAIN ................................... 44

CHAPTER FIVE – FOLK MAGICK ...................................................................... 52

CHAPTER SIX – LOVE AND MONEY ................................................................. 60

CHAPTER SEVEN – CANDLE MAGIC ............................................................... 78

CHAPTER EIGHT – MAGICK CRYSTALS AND PRECIOUS STONES ............. 94

CHAPTER NINE – HERBS: NATURES GIFT .................................................... 130

CHAPTER TEN – THE MAGICK PENDULUM .................................................. 148

CHAPTER ELEVEN – MAGICK FROM AROUND THE WORLD ..................... 155

# BECOME A SUPER-BEING

*In the mind of every thinking person there is set aside a special room, a museum of wonders. Every time we enter that museum we find our attention gripped by marvel number one, this strange Universe, in which we live and move and have our being.*

John A. Wheeler

# BECOME A SUPER-BEING

## Introduction

**IT** had been more than a week since the old man had left his bed. Instinctively he knew that he would soon be leaving the material world behind. He knew the time to pass on the secrets that he had spent a lifetime learning was short. Secrets that transcended recorded human history. Secrets that were as old as the universe, maybe even older. If he died before he could teach someone else his mysteries, they would all be lost forever; a fate the old man was not willing to except.

I hadn't known the old man for long, no more than a year or so. He had been a college professor once. He had worn a lot of faces over his long years. The world had been at his beck and call in the days when everything still retained mysteries.

He finally retired to live in quiet reflection in the small college town where he once taught. That's where I met him. He still actively volunteered his time by assisting professors and tutoring students who found the mysteries of the world too much for their young minds to bear.

I don't know why he picked me. I was by no means the best student he was tutoring. My major was in broadcasting and journalism. This class was strictly a required course, meant to be taken and quickly forgotten. The old man, however, must have seen something in me that was not obvious at the time. A spark in my soul perhaps. He never explained his choice, he simply said that I was the one and left it at that. Who was I to question his decision?

It was obvious that he would not recover from his illness. So, I reluctantly agreed to hear his story and learn his mysteries. Little did I realize it was a decision that would forever change my life. The knowledge that he had finally found his apprentice seemed to put new vigor in the old man's withered frame.

In the few short weeks that followed I heard amazing stories of lost civilizations and the natural laws of the universe that could only be described as magic and mysticism. I learned of mysterious, invisible energies that surround and permeate our very essence.

# BECOME A SUPER-BEING

I was taught about the strange spiritual beings that share our world and our lives. Mysteries of the ages were revealed to me, and it was my responsibility to use these secrets to help mankind and to further its spiritual evolution.

My mind was reeling. So much knowledge had been crammed into my brain in such a short period of time that I was experiencing information overload. For two weeks I had been spending every available minute with the old man, learning everything my poor brain could handle.

I had to get away.

The weekend arrived, and I used the excuse of going home to visit my parents to get a break from his teachings. The old man understood perfectly, and bade me farewell. He had taught me everything he could. Now, he too, could finally go home.

At the end of the weekend I arrived back to my sleepy little college ready to take on the next wave of learning. When I went to continue my lessons I was met by a locked door and foreboding silence.

I knew that something had happened; that something was different.

It really came as no shock when a friendly neighbor quietly informed me that the old man had passed away in his sleep the day after I left. He had been found by the visiting nurse who helped him with his daily regimen of medicines.

The old man's funeral was a quiet affair attended by a few acquaintances and fellow professors. He left this world much in the same way he lived in it; with quiet dignity and aplomb. The gift he left to me and the world, however, seemed far too special for such a modest, unassuming man to have acquired over one, short lifetime.

I have often wondered over the years if my friend had lived more than one life on this planet. Was it possible that he could have been known by many different names in many different lands? This was one secret the old man took with him on his last journey.

The secrets and mysteries taught to me by my friend were not meant to remain hidden forever. In his last days the old man had told me that mankind was reaching a turning point in its evolution. Mankind had arrived at a crossroad in its development. The direction it chose to follow would determine whether humans would continue to spiritually develop as children of God and the universe; or destroy themselves and be lost forever.

This book is my attempt to pass on to the world a small portion of what I was taught concerning the mysteries of our reality. This book is more than cute magic spells and charms. It is a philosophy of life for the children of planet Earth; whose final destiny is the universe and all the secrets and mysteries it contains within.

# BECOME A SUPER-BEING

## CHAPTER ONE – WHAT IS ALCHEMY?

**FOR** many, the word Alchemy conjures up images of medieval magicians trying to discover the secrets of transmuting common metals into valuable gold. Indeed, many manuscripts were written over the centuries detailing experiments in the quest to discover the mysteries of precious elements.

However, Alchemy was more than just a way to obtain material wealth. It was a way to obtain something much more valuable, spiritual wealth. The most common misconception about Alchemy is that it was exclusively the precursor to modern chemistry and had as its sole objective the transmutation of base metals into gold.

Although chemistry did evolve from Alchemy; the mysterious dogma of Alchemy pertains more to the quest for the Elixir of life, the Key to immortality and health, and the search for the Stone of Knowledge. Alchemy is a multifaceted subject. No longer can it be seen merely as a kind of pre-chemistry dominated by the desire to make gold, or prepare an elixir that would prolong life. This view would confine Alchemy to historical interest only.

The wide range of different ideas and perspectives found in alchemical literature, both in printed books and manuscripts, show that Alchemy in many ways holds philosophies and ways of looking at the world that are still entirely relevant to us today.

Genuine Alchemy takes two basic forms: first, the exploration concerning the transforming of matter; and, second, the psychological mystical. The secret of the first form is the interaction between the alchemist and the substance undergoing transformation by chemical or other means. That is, the alchemist in a occult way, aids the transformations that bring about the creation of an Elixir of Immortality.

For the alchemist, following this form of Alchemy, the changing of base metals into gold was only a stage on the way to the ultimate goal. The second form of Alchemy pertains to changing the alchemist. This requires following certain specific and often complicated procedures. The aim is "Adeptship," the emergence of a new individual from the ashes of the old. The ultimate goal is still immortality, but a directly achieved one, rather than the creation of an elixir which is taken by the alchemist over a period of time. The exact nature of this immortality was often the subject of heated discussions.

## Children Of The Universe

To understand Alchemy, the first thing to remember is that all elements came into being at the beginning of this universe. Matter and energy change form, but no new matter has been created since the beginning of time. This means, in the words of the late Carl Sagan, "that you are made of star stuff." Your spirit and thought energy, and every atom in your body have been in existence since the beginning of time.

We are children of the universe. Made from space dust that was swirling in space long before the earth or the solar system was formed. This is why the movement of planets can have an effect on people's emotions. Just as the moon and its monthly cycles affects the tidal seas and the life of all plants and animals.

The way that the universal elements and spiritual energies behave is very much the subject of Alchemy. Alchemists make use of all forms of cosmic energy, spiritual energy, and elixirs, for long life, good health, and harmony of mind. Supposedly, Alchemists also have a good reputation for creating effective spells, charms and amulets.

It has been observed that when a person thinks and feels lucky, then that person will actually begin to attract luck. The fact that so many rich and successful people own and believe in charms, seems to support this theory. However, is it simply belief, or can it actually be mind over matter at work? Alchemy has always had many faces. It has never been exclusively about the practical working with substances, but always had a spiritual and mystical aspect.

# BECOME A SUPER-BEING

Many writers even addressed important religious ideas as related to Alchemy. Some of the earliest alchemical manuscripts are concerned primarily with spiritual or mystical matters. For example, the Buchder Heiligen Dreifaltigkeit, one of the earliest German alchemical manuscripts (dated to 1515), deals with parallels between Christ and the alchemical process. These Christian parallels are also explored by the very influential Siebmacher's Waterstone of the Wise, which went through a staggering 14 editions.

Paracelsus (1493 1541), the great reformer of alchemy, also wrote on religious and spiritual matters, and his influence on late 16th and 17th century alchemy was profound. During the early 17th century Jacob Boehme (1575 1624) wrote a number of mystical works, some of which drew on Paracelsist alchemical ideas, **The Signaturum Rerum, the Threefold life of Man, and the Four Complexions.** These were published throughout the 17th century and developed a new thread of mysticism, with alchemical resonances.

In many alchemical works the mystical and physical threads are so closely interwoven that it is not possible to separate them. For many alchemists, the mystical was alive, ingrained in the material world, and the alchemical transmutation process was for them a kind of mystical purification. Yet, Alchemy is still best known for its search for material riches.

Writer Vicki Davies believes that Alchemy was more than a speculative art; it was also an operative art. Since the time of the immortal Hermes, alchemists have asserted that they could manufacture gold from tin, silver, lead and mercury. Many intellectuals delved into the secrets of alchemy: Thomas Norton, Basil Valentine, Albertus Magnus, Paracelsus, Nicholas Flammel, Comte de St. Germain, Raymund Lully, and Count Bernard of Treviso. Legends attest that both King Solomon and Pythagoras were alchemists and that the former manufactured by alchemical means the gold used in his temple.

Alchemy, the secret art of the land of Khem (Egypt), is one of the two oldest sciences known to the world. Its beginnings extend back into the obscurity of prehistoric times. According to the earliest records extant, Alchemy was considered as divinely revealed to man so that by their aid he might regain his lost estate.

Some say that Alchemy was revealed to man by the mysterious demigod Hermes Trismegistus in his Emerald Tablet. Here one finds the oldest and most revered of all the alchemical formula. It relates both to the Alchemy of the base metals and the divine Alchemy of human regeneration.

Hermes is credited by the Egyptians as being the author of all the great arts and sciences. In honor of him, all scientific knowledge was gathered under the general title of The Hermetic Arts. Alchemy is the science of multiplication and is based upon the natural phenomenon of growth.

"Nothing from nothing comes" is an extremely ancient adage. Alchemy is not the process of making something from nothing; it is the process of increasing and improving that which already exists. Alchemy teaches that God is in everything, that he is one universal spirit, manifesting through an infinity of forms. God, therefore, is the spiritual seed planted in the dark earth.

By art, it is possible to grow and expand this seed so that the entire universe of substance is tinctured and becomes like the seed pure gold. In the spiritual nature of man this is termed regeneration. In the material body of the elements, it is called transmutation. As it is in the spiritual and material universes, so it is in the intellectual world. Through art (the process of learning) the whole mass of base metals, (the mental body of ignorance), was transmuted into pure gold (wisdom), for it was tinctured with understanding. Through faith and proximity to God the consciousness of man may be transmuted from base animal desires, (represented by the masses of the planetary metals), into a pure, golden, and godly consciousness. If also the base metals of mental ignorance can be transmuted into genius and wisdom, then why not also can the material elements of the universe be multiplied? That which is above is also below.

If alchemy be a great spiritual fact, then it is also a great material fact. If it can take place in the universe, it can take place in man and it can also take place in the plants and minerals. The general aim of alchemists was to carry out in the laboratory, as far as possible, the processes which Nature carried out in the interior of the Earth.

***The preparation of a compound named elixir, or philosopher's stone which possessed the property of transmuting the baser metals into gold and silver.***

# BECOME A SUPER-BEING

*The creation of homunculi, or living beings. The preparation of a universal solvent which dissolved every substance which was immersed in it.*

*Palingenesis, or the restoration of a plant from its ashes.*

*The preparation of spiritus mundi, a mystic substance possessing many powers, the principal of which was its capacity of dissolving gold.*

*The extraction of the quintessence or active principle of all substances.*

*The preparation of aurum potable, liquid gold. Gold itself being perfect could produce perfection in the human frame.*

In Alchemy, there are three symbolic substances: mercury, sulphur and salt. To these was added a fourth mysterious life principle called Azoth. The mercury, sulphur and salt referred to are not to be confused with the crude salt, sulphur and mercury taken from the earth or bought from a chemist. They each have a triune nature because each substance contains the other two. Salt therefore contains salt (predominantly), mercury and sulphur. Likewise the other two.

These nine divisions three times three, (three elements or processes in three worlds divine, human and elemental, plus Azoth equals 10, the sacred decade of Pythagoras. To some, Azoth, the mysterious universal life force, is the invisible, eternal fire or electricity or magnetism or astral light. Azoth could actually be the Unified Field. The alchemist must do his work in four worlds at the same time to achieve the Magnum Opus.

An example follows: The Triune Power in Four Worlds.

# BECOME A SUPER-BEING

*World of Father, Son, Mother*
*1. God, father, Son, Holy Ghost*
*2. Man, Spirit, Soul, Body*
*3. Elements, Air, Fire, Water*
*4. Chemicals, Mercury, Sulphur, Salt*

The alchemical philosophers used the symbols of salt, sulphur, and mercury to represent not only chemicals but the spiritual and invisible principles of God, man, and the universe. These three substances existing in four worlds sum up to the sacred number twelve. These twelve are the foundations of the Great Work (the search for the inner gold), for alchemists.

In Alchemy is found the perpetuation of the Universal Mystery. Alchemists believe that as surely as Jesus died upon the cross, so in Alchemy, unless the elements first die, the great work cannot be achieved.

The stages of the alchemical processes can be traced in the lives and activities of nearly all the world saviors and teachers. It is said in the Bible that "except a man be born again, he cannot see the kingdom of God."

In Alchemy it is declared that without putrefaction the great work cannot be accomplished. What is it that dies on the cross or becomes black with putrefaction or does this same thing to the nature of man so that he may rise again? The solution in the alchemical retort, if digested a certain length of time, will turn into a red elixir, which is called the universal medicine or philosopher's stone. It resembles a fiery water and is luminous in the dark. When it is properly developed, this universal solvent in liquid form will dissolve into itself all other metals.

In this high state, the universal salt is a liquid fire. This salt dissolved with the proper amount of any metal and run through the different stages of digestion and rotations of augmentations will eventually become a medicine for the transmuting of inferior metals.

In classifying the processes through which the chemical elements must pass before the Hermetic or universal medicine is produced, the Dictionnaire Mytho Hermetique lists twelve: Calcination, congelation, fixation, dissolution, digestion, distillation, sublimation, separation, incineration, fermentation, multiplication, projection.

These twelve steps lead to the accomplishment of the Magnus Opus or "secret essence."

One of the great alchemists observed that man's quest for gold is often his undoing for the mistakes the alchemical processes believing them to be purely material. He does not realize that the Philosopher's Stone, the Philosopher's Gold and the Philosopher's Medicine exist in each of the four worlds and that the consummation of the experiment cannot be realized until it is successfully carried on in four worlds simultaneously according to one formula. Furthermore, one of the constituents of the alchemical formula exists only within the nature of man himself, without which his chemicals will not combine.

A person who wants to be an alchemist must have in himself the "magnesia" or the magnetic power to attract and "coagulate" invisible astral elements. Thus the one performing the experiments must him/her self be a Magus. Unless the greater alchemy has first taken place within the soul of man, he cannot perform the lesser alchemy in the retort. Thus, the genuine alchemists looked into the dross of man to refine it into its higher life.

The secret of the alchemical art is said to be contained in the aphoristic principle "solve et coagula" "dissolve and combine." This is a fair description of the physical aspect of the alchemical process: at each stage, the various characteristics of a substance are stripped away, and a new, nobler substance is built up. In a spiritual aspect, this means a "death" and "rebirth."

In the final stage of **The Great Work**, "the King is reunited in the Fire of Love with his blessed Queen" and the Alchemist becomes the perfect being, the Divine Androgyny, the perfect conjunction of man and woman (the Chemical Marriage).

## Documented Evidence

Hundreds of journals and manuscripts detailing the experiments of alchemists have survived the centuries. These papers seem to indicate that some alchemists were successful in their goal of transmutation. One such document is

# BECOME A SUPER-BEING

the testimony of the Monk Albertus Bayr who claimed to have discovered transmutation through evoking a spirit.

*I, Frater Albertus Bayr, of the Order of the Carmelites, hereby testify before God that in the Year 1568, on the 18th of February, the Feast of the Purification of the Virgin Mary, in my Cell in the monastery of Maria Magdalena de Stella Nova, such a Countenance appeared to me and held converse with me.*

*I had risen and retired to bed with philosophical books and thoughts; day and night I had prayed fervently to our Lord God to reveal to me the Truth of this art. Then, in my ignorance, and may God forgive me, I knew not what else to do. With great assiduity I had labored in vain for three and twenty years with my abbot and by Day and by Night had diligently tended the fire. So I thought that one could learn this Mystery from no man and must wrest it from the Spirits. Yet, as, praised be God, I learned in the end, more is possible to Men than to Spirits.*

*So did I on that day begin with the Ceremonies and Exorcisms of Italian Spanish monks. As the exorcist of the monastery, God forgive me, I then called the Spirit of the Planet Mercury, and demanded that it should speak and answer. In the shape of a dark and elongated Disc, a Shadow without definite Contour, did it appear to me and in ringing and resounding Tones permit Question and Answer.*

*At its Bidding I sat down at the table, in order with pen and ink to record the Truth. Then the Shadow, the black Gleam, entered into the middle of the Circle. The blessed sword, the consecrated candles, and the rest of the magic, did not hold it from entering.*

*Slowly it changed from Black through ashen grey clouds to a bright white Gleam, and at last it was transformed from the White, through a shining yellow color, into the most glorious Red. Form and Contours, however, changed not, and stood immovable until the end of the conversation in the Magic Circle. But in the middle of the gleam the Sign of Mercurius appeared in changing colors.*

*When it disappeared, my cell was lit up within and without blood red, and it was as when the Sun appears blood red in a room.*

*After this Revelation I settled everything with my Abbot, and with Labor and Diligence procured within two years eleven pounds and three and a half ounces of the right Material. Anno 1571 I had completed the Work and truly and clearly set it down. But my Abbot did not live to see it. On the Second of June preceding he was found dead in bed alongside his Concubine. From the Beginning to the End of the Work I saw all colors, as revealed by the Spirit in the Circle.*

*Three main colors did I find in the Work Black, White and Red. And when a mistake occurred, I received counsel and information from the Spirit. But after completing the Work, I have not for years been able to summon the Spirit.*

*Therefore the improvement in quality and quantity has been very difficult for me. And as the other brethren and in especial the new Abbot were very hostile to me, because they could not learn the Secret from me, a few years later I went privily on my way. With my Tincture and a few ancient good Egyptian books I came safely to Augsburg. Thereafter I traveled towards Nuremberg, and rejoiced to be finally back on German Soil.*

*I am consoled by the hope of soon finding one who will show to me the Improving and Increasing. May God Almighty help all in His mercy. Be He praised evermore. Amen.*

*Figulus, Benedictus. Rosarium novum Olympicum et benedictum. Das ist: ein newer gebenedeyter philosophischer Rosengarten..., Basel, 1608.*

## Spiritual Alchemy

The science of physics and chemistry can trace their roots back to Alchemy and the alchemists who delved into its mysteries. However, there is a whole body of alchemical thought that has ignored the physical aspects of Alchemy, instead, embracing Alchemy exclusively for its spiritual nature. This movement surfaced in the nineteenth century with a number of alchemical scholars, including Ethan Allen Hitchcock.

In 1857, Hitchcock published Alchemy and the Alchemists, a book that proposed a revolutionary modern interpretation of the ancient Hermetic art, but nevertheless, harked back to alchemy's origins. Hitchcock's argument was that the transmutation of metals was never Alchemy's true goal but was instead a symbol of humanity's struggle toward spiritual salvation.

# BECOME A SUPER-BEING

Hitchcock's book presented convincing evidence that all alchemical references stood for elements of the human soul. For example, mercury - the fluid metal that "yearned" toward gold – was a symbol of human consciousness, yearning for spiritual perfection. Hitchcock maintained that alchemists expressed their ideas in obscure alchemical terms in order to avoid religious persecution. Alchemists believed that people should become enlightened by self-discovery.

This flew in the face of Church authorities, who thought that coercion and violence might be legitimately employed to force men into the established public faith. According to Hitchcock, the alchemists' efforts were only partially successful, for by saving "their own heads," they "plunged hundreds and thousands of the 'profane' into vain and useless efforts to find a tangible agent for turning the baser metals into gold."

Hitchcock's speculations survive today as more people are drawn to the ancient truths that reveal how humankind can "transmute" their bodies, their souls, their universal essence into the creation reality. When this is known, people will discover how malleable the world around them really is.

## Modern Alchemy

Alchemy is alive and well today. There are many practicing alchemists living throughout the world. Some were trained at the Paracelsus College located in Salt Lake City, Utah in the 1960's and 70's by Frater Albertus. In Frater Albertus's laboratories, disciples practiced a "three-fold process of separation" on herbs and succulents, extracting the "soul" and "spirit" and burning the leftovers to purify the "body." These three "essentials" were reconstituted into a substance called plant stone, which, according to a complex correspondence between the original plant and specific parts of the body, served as a powerful medicine.

After the death of Frater Albertus in 1984 some of his followers went on to other alchemical pursuits. Alchemy is isolating the principle of life i.e. the vital force. Once this is isolated, it can be further processed to make an elixir of immortality.

Alchemists strive towards being one with God. What the alchemist does in his laboratory is exactly the same process that is done in any therapy or metaphysical training program. The differences between the systems are what you separate what are considered essential how much do you purify and when do you stop the process or when is the cohabitation or unification?

Western Alchemy provides the earliest clear cut paradigm of co creation. In fact, this was the supreme telos of the Mysteries, and the theogenesis (immortality), was merely the method of preparing for it. In fact, it was widely known that the result of initiation into the Mysteries was immortality, the raising of the human being to the status of a living God endowed with super human faculties and powers of life extension. Part of the device of concealing the aim of the Mysteries was to "leak" the method as if it were the aim, but the western alchemists inherited the second part of the proposition which was never divulged.

The true purpose of the theogenesis was solely to fit the initiate for the sacred work of co creation. The Great Work, the Spagyric Art, the production of the Divine Hermaphrodite, the attainment of the Philosopher's Stone were all euphemisms for the task of co creation, the supreme act of divine service. Thus, theogenesis was the method and co creation the aim of alchemy.

Here, co-creation consisted of two phases: a process of restoration and a task of completion. The idea that creation God's creation on Earth, including all of nature and the human species is incomplete, and that the rightful sharing of humanity in the creative evolution of the world has been deviated by superhuman forces, were the most closely guarded teachings of the Mysteries.

## The Science Of Metaphysics

According to Stephen Michael Nanninga, in our modern age, the value of metaphysics is not generally taken seriously within the scientific community. This is understandable. The practice of philosophizing physical theory has no place in conventional science where theories and ideas must remain just that until verified objectively. However, as we come to understand what metaphysics actually is, we begin to realize that modern physics is metaphysics in a rediscovered and more perfected form.

Conventional science, the objectively knowable perspective on reality, and the entire Universe it describes, become recognized as expressions of a transcendental state of reality which, by virtue of its unchangeable unified condition, is even more real than the physical Universe itself.

The purpose of metaphysics is often misunderstood among religious thinkers. When a teaching becomes so dogmatic that it loses track of any sort of metaphysical understanding of the transcendental omnipresence, it becomes essentially stagnant and blind to what a spiritual universe is all about. Those familiar with the mystical philosophies of Alchemy do not have a problem with the abstract universal principles of metaphysics and how they relate to the restrictions of theological traditions. Ideally, the ultimate goal of any theological tradition should be to bring the individual seeker to a state of spiritual awareness in which all such theological traditions are assimilated, and at the same time, not needed in their dogmatic form.

Much has been written in recent years about the enlightening parallels between modern physical theory and ancient metaphysics. Not only is science finding it increasingly difficult to keep itself separated from philosophical speculation, but as we develop our abstract understanding of the universe as a whole, the fields of physics and metaphysics seem to be losing their distinction altogether.

More than ever, as we examine our field of space-time from every possible perspective, we probe our consciousness for the mystical truth. With our great pride in scientific knowledge, have we ignorantly filed the most beautiful principles of ancient mysticism into the category of the absurd? In our secular materialism and religious zeal, have we forgotten the real substance of the ancient message?

Have we forgotten the true meaning of reality? Yet, perhaps we are not so lost after all. Perhaps we are at the dawn of a great awakening, a great remembering, something which has been in the making for a very long time. It is for you, of course, to think and decide for yourself.

Explore the traditions and directions that draw your interest. Trust your intuition. The most beautiful mystical realizations are both strangely bizarre and profoundly simple. It is often said that the ancient wisdom of Alchemy takes only moments to teach, yet lifetimes to understand. This is the greatest quest there is.

# BECOME A SUPER-BEING

# BECOME A SUPER-BEING

## CHAPTER TWO – THE NATURE OF REALITY

### *What is the mind? No Matter. What is Matter? Never Mind.*

**WHEN** astronomers observe the Andromeda Galaxy, our nearest galactic neighbor, they are actually seeing a galaxy that existed more than 2 million years ago. This is because light is not instantaneous, it travels at about 186,000 miles per second. While this is extremely fast, it still takes time to travel through the vast distances of space. This means that the farther we look into space, the further back in time we are seeing. This also means that space and time are interwoven into a single continuum know as space-time.

Looking deeper into space, the realm of the galaxy gradually gives way to the realm of the quasar, a mysterious object with the mass and energy of an entire galaxy, concentrated into a relativity small spherical volume, about the size of our solar system. It was once assumed that the quasar was an early form of the galaxy, but how galaxies actually form and how quasars fit in to the evolutionary scheme of the universe is still not understood.

Recent observations indicate that many quasars actually exist within host galaxies, and are powered by black holes. As we gaze into the blackness of infinity itself, we are actually looking at the beginning of the universe. The diverging field of infinity all around us, the experience of infinity, is like a reversed image of the Universal Singularity, the Big Bang.

This popular name is actually incorrect because the cosmic creation was nothing like an explosion. It would have been more like the intense force field experienced near the singularity of a black hole. The entire history of the universe is encoded into the most basic components of our bodies, so as strange as it may

# BECOME A SUPER-BEING

seem, we are actually not far removed from the beginning of the universe even at this very moment.

The conditions in the earliest stages of the universe would be very similar to the conditions we would find right now deep within any atom, in the quantum realm. As one looks at the stuff of the universe, it's striking how out of chaos, order is formed, how out of dreams becomes reality. When we consider how special conditions that seem to favor the development of life appear to be built into the laws of reality, it is hard not to speculate that there is some intelligent order in the vast complexities of the universe. The universe actually provides us with the tools to understand the mystery of the ages, why? Because the knowledge is our lost legacy, and once regained the universe will once again be complete.

## Quantum Reality

We now know that energy and matter are one and the same and so are space-time. Einstein's formula $E=MC^2$ showed that matter can become energy and vice versa. If we observe reality for being one side of the thought equation, then the other side must be perception. Perception with enough will becomes a new reality.

Every time a new idea is set forth and enough people believe it to be true, it actually become true. Just as the belief that some of these theories have determinable flaws based on the physical universe. Others perceive new views of the universe where those physical limitations no longer exist, opening the way for a new reality.

One recent example of this kind of thinking is Quantum theory. The grand unifying causality of the universe must include the primal forces of the universe: energy, matter, space, time, reality and thought. The unifying causality can be considered the original creative energy of the universe, the force that many consider God. It must also be realized that all that we are, our body, mind and spirit are reflections of this original force, looking to reconnect and reunite.

Many believe that the universe will collapse back on itself recombining into the original force. This may happen when enough of our thoughts pull us all together to create a new thought based on grand unifying reality for the universe, and once again we will be of a singularity, for we are all of one great idea.

Einstein suggested that the speed of light was not only finite, but must also be constant, regardless of the motion of any observer. This was necessary in order to make any logical sense out of physical causality, the whole experience of what causes what is space-time and the very experience of time itself. However, since this logical causality for an observer is defined by light coming from objects, and other observers have other light coming to them over a different path through space-time, a very strange condition is imposed, any objective view of the universe must be entirely observer dependent, and there is no real basis for the notion of a true universal time frame.

Every one of us has our very own light cone which defines for us the present state of the universe, along with what we experience as logical causality and even the passage of time. Every light cone is different, so no one can ever exactly agree on what is happening where or when. Of course, the differences are small except under relativistic conditions, such as near the speed of light, or the singularity of a black hole. However, they are real and they are there, all the time.

The "where-when's" of space-time are relative. In fact, since everything we see in space, from our own bodies to the distant quasars, are images from the past, the actual present state of the universe is never seen. The scientist must make a clear distinction between "that which appears to be" and "that which actually is."

Strangely, everything seems to fall into the former category. For most of this century, science has been struggling with some very strange revelations uncovered by relativity and quantum theory. These insights have shown us that the basic ideas we have about objective reality are very limited views of what the universe is really like. The reason they were such a struggle for science is that they blew away the foundational framework of classical physics, and our entire understanding of physical reality, in a most fundamental and definite way. Could it be that our fundamental assumptions about space and time are simply not correct? Perhaps we have yet to realize the value in the most beautiful and mysterious experience of all. The experience of consciousness.

There is a persistent view of the material world in which every object is composed of atoms, which in turn are composed of other particles, the subatomic particles, and those which cannot be divided any further, are called elementary particles, or quanta. This is true in a limited sense, but the more we come to understand just what quanta are, the more we begin to see how limited this view is.

First of all, matter and energy are both composed of quanta, and are today considered to be merely two different aspects of the same thing, which could be called, in the tradition of space-time, matter-energy. Even the classical distinction between a particle and a wave becomes fuzzy in the quantum realm, and quanta are often referred to as wavicles. Wavicles, whatever they are, are only a hint at the latest understanding of subatomic reality.

In relativistic quantum field theory, a quantum is more properly thought of as a quantum process, and whether it displays the properties of a wave or a particle, it is considered to be a manifestation of an underlying field. The quantum field is the primary reality, and it is through the manifestation of quanta that we experience this underlying reality, which is entirely ethereal. This ethereal reality seems to be governed entirely by thoughts and observation. The atom is best described as a dynamic system of quantum processes, a resonating pattern of interacting force fields. The closer we look into the atom, which is the job of the particle accelerators, the more intense these processes become, and the more any notion of solidity seems to "zoom away" to a deeper level.

Mathematically, today's model of the atom is built from multidimensional gauge fields and vector bundles, a sort of "emptiness" full of ethereal symmetries. The whole experience of the solidity of matter arises from the mutual repulsion of negatively charged electron fields. It is a surface illusion. Even the electron itself is not solid. Like all quantum particles, it is treated mathematically as a singularity, and it is entirely impossible to pin it down as an "object in space-time."

It is now generally accepted that this ethereal nature of matter is not merely a mathematical limitation of physical theory, but is in fact a deeply fundamental characteristic of physical reality. One of the most recent theories describes matter and energy as 11 dimensional fields rolled into quantum sized spheres, tubes, and strings. Even the vacuum of space is considered to be literally filled with quantum activity.

# BECOME A SUPER-BEING

## The Multiverse

One major school of quantum theory suggests a multiplicity of universes. A simple experiment, familiar to every student of physics, involves light passing through slits in a barrier; its results, according to Oxford physicist Deutsch, lead inevitably to the idea that there are countless universes parallel to our own, through which some of the light must pass.

This "many worlds" interpretation of quantum theory has gained advocates in recent years, and Deutsch argues that it is time for scientists to face the full implications of this idea. To that end, he outlines a new view of the Multiverse (the total of all the parallel universes). He argues effectively that quantum computation, a discipline in which he is a pioneering thinker, has the potential for building computers that draw on their counterparts in parallel universes; this could make true artificial intelligence a reality. Likewise, time travel into both the future and the past should be possible, though not in quite the form envisioned by science fiction writers; the trips would almost certainly be one way, and they would likely take the travelers into different universes from the one they originally began in.

Our "local realistic" view of the world assumes that phenomena are separated by time and space and that no influence can travel faster than the speed of light. Quantum non-locality proves that these assumptions are incorrect, and that there is a principle of holistic interconnectedness operating at the quantum level which contradicts the localistic assumptions of classical, Newtonian physics. At the subatomic level, matter does not exist with certainty at definite places, but rather shows "tendencies to exist," and atomic events do not occur with certainty at definite times and in definite ways, but rather show "tendencies to occur."

At the quantum level, "particles" do not possess definite, deterministic qualities until they are observed and measured. Despite the fact that the quality of particles is unclear until a measurement is made, any two photons or electrons that originate from a common source will possess a total spin of zero once they are measured.

Quantum theory tells us that in a system of two particles having total spin of zero, the spins of the particles about any axis will always be correlated, even though they only exist as tendencies, or potentialities, before the measurement is taken. Because the spin of a particle does not exist until a measurement is made, the act of making the measurement and determining the axis of spin will determine the spin of particle one no matter how far apart it is from particle two. Particle two will instantly respond to the state of particle one, even if it is on the other side of the universe. At the instant we perform our measurement on particle one, particle two, which may be thousands of miles away, will acquire a definite spin "up" or "down."

How does particle two know which axis we have chosen? There is no time for it to receive that information by any conventional signal.

## Quantum Non-Locality

Quantum non-locality as suggested by Bell's theorem is a fact of nature that has now been experimentally verified on many occasions. Alain Aspect's experiments in 1982 at the University of Paris South proved the existence of quantum non-locality. These experiments have been refined and repeated many times since.

At the quantum level, instantaneous actions occur at a distance. Two particles that are part of a single system continue to act in concert with one another no matter how far apart they appear to be separated by space-time. Non-locality or non-separability is asking us to change completely our ideas about objects, to remove a popular projection we have upon nature.

We can no longer consider objects as independently existing entities that can be localized in well defined regions of space-time. They are interconnected in ways not even conceivable using ideas from classical physics, which is largely a refinement and approximation from our normal sense of functioning. Nature has shown us that our concept of reality, consisting of units that can be considered as separate from each other, is fundamentally wrong. For this reason, Bell's theorem may be the most profound discovery of science.

Quantum non-locality proves that particles that were once together in an interaction remain in some sense parts of a single system which responds together to further interactions. Since the entire universe originated in a flash of light known as the Big Bang, the existence of quantum non-locality points toward a profound cosmological holism and suggests that if everything that ever interacted in the Big Bang maintains its connection with everything it interacted with, then every particle in every star and galaxy that we can see "knows" about the existence of every other particle.

If every "particle" is in communication with every other "particle," could the phenomenon of quantum non-locality help account in some way for the self organizing, recurrent patterns of form that appear everywhere in the universe? Could such a theory contribute to our understanding of morphogenesis on a cosmological level?

The Greek philosopher Plotinus believed that the metaphysical principle of Mind is non-local, and explained that, because it is not limited by time and space, it can be present everywhere. Similarly, Karl Pribram has demonstrated that memory is not localized in specific parts of the brain. Does quantum non-locality support, or help us understand, noetic theories of the universe? Is the underlying structure of the universe essentially noetic in nature?

What is the nature of the universal "laws of physics," which seem to be the same everywhere. Do the laws of physics presuppose some type of non-locality? Does the very concept of "the universe" as one thing imply a form of cosmological holism and non-locality?

### The Magic Of Creation

The classical notion of empty space has been replaced with the concept of the quantum vacuum. Quantum theory allows for the probability that at any point in the vacuum a particle antiparticle pair will simply pop into existence, only to immediately annihilate each other again. In fact, this process is considered to actually be happening, everywhere. In the first marriage of quantum theory and relativity, particle physics and cosmology were combined when a black hole was placed in the quantum vacuum. The result was the startling realization that, through a very strange process, black holes actually emit energy, and the smaller they are, the hotter they shine. In some cases, they could even be indistinguishable from white holes, and in all cases, they eventually evaporate away to nothing.

# BECOME A SUPER-BEING

Probably the most intriguing realization of all to come out of quantum theory is the fact that there is some sort of connection between quanta that completely ignores space-time separation, even if the quanta are at opposite ends of the universe. Somehow, we must consider quanta as existing in a dimension in which nothing is separate. Exactly how this can be certainly defies logic, but it is real, it is as fundamental to physical reality as the quanta are themselves.

The experience of matter-energy in space-time demands a level of understanding that goes well beyond objective logic. Today's mathematical models of the quantum realm have implications that reach back to the earliest stages of the universe, yet they will never be objectively verified in the way classical Newtonian mechanics has been. It is simply not practical to do so. The scientist of today must rely on emerging patterns and hints experienced at the macroscopic level of the particle accelerators, and finally on the aesthetic beauty of the mathematics itself to help establish which direction to take toward truth. It would appear that we could say, Beauty is indeed Truth, and physics has become metaphysics.

## Ancient Teachings

Since before the current cycle of recorded history on this planet, the ancient message of non-dualistic mysticism has been passed down to us and preserved in various forms of expression and degrees of purity. While the universal principles involved are said to be profoundly simple, they are completely abstract and defy any sort of straight forward logical expression. Fortunately, the intuitive insight required to understand mystical principles is a special quality of the human mind.

The most fundamental principle of mysticism is transcendental omnipresence, which refers to being totally independent of space-time while still being everywhere at once in space-time. The idea of transcendental unity is built in to this principle, since we are referring to a single, undifferentiated state of being.

The second most fundamental principle is polarity, which refers to the inherent dynamic creative aspect of the transcendental state, and is said to be the essence of consciousness, both at the universal level and the individual level.

# BECOME A SUPER-BEING

From these simple principles the entire physical universe is manifest in all its cyclic diversity, from the highest frequencies of oscillating energy to the ellipses of orbiting planets, from the birth and death of stars to the expansion and possible collapse of the universe itself.

The scientific fields of cosmology and particle physics can at first seem to be remote and unimportant studies as far as the human condition is concerned, yet they actually provide insight into the nature of consciousness itself, our awareness of existence and how we perceive it. Most intriguing, objective science has uncovered a unified state of the universe, a higher dimension that exists in its unified state at this very moment.

Our consciousness, our bodies, and every last particle in the universe are an inseparable part of this higher dimension, as if the physical world were merely a "transient projection" of a pristine higher realm that always exists and never changes. Is unified field physics a physical theory realization of a transcendental omnipresence? Is such "cosmic awareness" actually illuminating our spiritual dimension within a spiritual universe?

These questions, of course, will never be answered by physical theory. They are intrinsically beyond the reach of objective expression. It is increasingly obvious, however, that such questions will also never be rendered impractical by physical theory, which instead is laying the possibilities clearly in the open. The fact that we are actually in a position to see modern physics as a rediscovery of ancient metaphysics is a measure of mankind's open minded progress in spite of our shortcomings and missteps along the way. It has been known for a very long time that objective communication does not lend itself to a precise expression of transcendental concept.

There is no question that an awakening is occurring on our planet. Earth is experiencing a particularly important period of transformation, and we must "get our act together" for a new age of spiritual awareness. The most fundamental problems of the human condition can be attributed to nothing but the ignorance of who we really are, a condition called, in Sanskrit, avidya. The problems were expected, the separateness and solidity of the physical realm is particularly convincing. However, now is the time to awaken to an intuitive understanding of the statement mystics have used for ages to confound the logical mind: "There is only That (transcendental omnipresence); we are That."

# BECOME A SUPER-BEING

We may be re-learning a very ancient system of spiritual knowledge, but we have the opportunity to understand it on an entirely new and conceptually very clear level. The essence of mystical knowledge resonates with our deepest level of being, yet it persistently defies our logic oriented minds. Normal objective logic is based on the knowledge of material separateness, and as far as our everyday existence is concerned, this is what reality is.

To the ancient mystics, this is the classical trap, to live in the material world means losing awareness of the greater "spiritual" world around us. The physical level of experience is that part of our being which makes us think we are separate, when in reality we are not, and if we think it is the only way of being, we have fallen into the trap of the ego self.

We have become so fully attached to the physical realm, that we tend to think of our body as our only means of selfness. This causes us, for example, to fear death, because we have essentially no awareness of our multi dimensional reality and those existence's of being which are independent of the physical body. For example, think of a television set. The picture does not originate from within the set. If the TV is broken, the signal is not destroyed, only the receiver. Our bodies are like TV sets, our essence transcends the body, destroy the body and our essence, the spirit, continues on. The material world is transient, things come and go. To the mystic, all forms of impermanence are a type of non reality, and for this reason we find in many of the ancient teachings the physical level being referred to as illusion. We see its true form in a illusory sense.

There is no doubt that the physical experience is real. If we walk into a brick wall, it hurts. However, the pain will pass, the wound will heal, and the wall will eventually crumble. What is important to realize is that through all the experiences of change, the true reality which underlies the physical world does not change. That level of reality which never changes is the most real, everything else is temporary and illusory.

One of the most distinctive facets of being human is being a distinct focus of consciousness, separated from what we perceive. Sometimes it is like staring out of a black sack with two holes in it. Many, perhaps most people are not always entirely comfortable with this separate existence as individuals. At times we yearn to be reunited, but we are not sure with what. Mystics in all religions have attempted to overcome this separation and achieve unity with the source of being: God, Allah, the Tao, Brahma, emptiness. Regardless of the religion, there

## BECOME A SUPER-BEING

are echoes among the diverse accounts of mystic experience. The central experience is one of overcoming the gap between self and unity. It is an experience often accompanied with ecstasy, and a sense of being in contact with ultimate reality. It is from the universe and from nature that we are separated. It is with the universe and with nature that we must eventually seek reunion.

# BECOME A SUPER-BEING

# BECOME A SUPER-BEING

## CHAPTER THREE—THE POWER OF THE MIND

*The most beautiful experience we can have is the mysterious. It is the fundamental emotion that stands at the cradle of true art and true science.*

### Albert Einstein

**ANCIENT** mysticism teaches that space-time and consciousness are polar aspects of each other. The entire field of space-time is like a reversed image of consciousness, matter is literally mind stuff. This is the subject object polarity. Just as on the objective side the universe is an unending process of space time continuum, so also on the subjective side pure consciousness is an unceasing stream of self transcendence.

Individual consciousness has a depth of extension equal to that of the universe itself. As incredible as this may seem, it is a very real metaphysical reality, the depth of space is a direct reflection of the depth of consciousness. The dimension of depth consciousness is transcendental, and we do not see its magnitude of extension as such. It is like viewing a line end on, appearing as a singularity in three dimensional space, with the length of the line not perceived at all. Indeed, this dimension cannot be seen because it is what we see with, it is experienced as the force of consciousness, life itself.

The polarity of consciousness is the very same polarity that we experience as time, and space is its polar aspect projected outward. In other words: we do not live in time, but time lives within us; because time is the innermost rhythm of our conscious existence, which appears outside of ourselves as space. We could also say: Space is the possibility of movement, time the actuality or the realization of movement. With this ancient understanding of space, time, and consciousness firmly in mind, we can look at the Big Bang in a different light.

# BECOME A SUPER-BEING

From a mystical perspective, the Big Bang of modern cosmology is a continuous process, an omnipresent condition which has always been the same no matter what we believed. Western science, caught up in its purely objective view of existence, has imposed the concept of "universal time" on this timeless condition, projecting it into the past. Mankind has completely ignored the ancient message of non-dualistic mysticism resulting in our science of the universe being bogged down in the "strangeness" of relativity and quantum theory for most of this century.

We have certainly developed an extraordinary understanding of the physical universe, and this was no doubt the purpose of modern science, but perhaps now is a good time to reintegrate the sacred science of the ancients. Best of all, a mystical understanding of modern cosmology sheds a good deal of light on the strange aspects of both modern physics and ancient mysticism.

## When You Wish Upon A Star...

Because of our direct connection with the universe and reality, our consciousness can subtly influence the day to day activities that normally seem beyond our control. For most of us our minds are wild and undisciplined. Our thoughts shoot from one subject to another with little or no conscious constraint. However, our thoughts are actually governing our reality and what will occur in our lives.

Because most of our thoughts are chaotic and random, so too are our daily lives. We can be the masters of our destiny, it just takes a little will-power and self-discipline. This is the great secret of the ancient alchemists. The hidden knowledge of Alchemy reveals that consciousness is the ultimate energy in the universe.

With this energy anything is possible. From the transmutation of base metals into pure gold, to the transmutation of the human mind into the next step in evolution, that of pure, unbounded energy. This is not as difficult as it appears, all we have to do is wake up. Everything in life is only as difficult as you think it is.

# BECOME A SUPER-BEING

Low self esteem has become especially prevalent in the U.S. Why? Externalized reasons are often suggested by people as to why they are the way they are, deprived childhood, no money, bad breaks in life or simply the people around them. Yet, in every deprived situation, there are noticeable individuals that have had meager beginnings and nevertheless develop stable, happy lives.

As one grows in self awareness, the realization slowly unfolds that one's own condition is brought about by oneself and one's own choices in life, whether they are gut reactive, knee jerk choices or conscious choices. Whatever you were dealt with at birth, your choices throughout your life determine your outcome. The more complete the usage of both your mind and body, the more physically and mentally able you become, and the better you feel about yourself.

## Thought Forms

Your words influence your thoughts. By thoughts we attune ourselves. The Power of love thoughts, harmonious thought, harmonious frequency. The more we think love thoughts the more we receive love thoughts. If we dwell on negative thoughts then negative experiences are what we will receive. The rule of the game is: thoughts are reality. Your feelings will tell you If you are creating what you want, or what you don't want. If you feel good, you create good things, if you feel bad, you create bad things. So if you are dwelling on something that makes you feel bad, you are creating negative thought forms.

Changing the focus of your thoughts changes your reality. If you are finally ready to stop living your life in a chaotic fashion, then here is an effective, yet simple, method to begin mastery of your reality. Take a goal or something that you have been wanting to happen. Try and visualize what it is you want. Don't just think about your goal in "verbal" terms, try to picture in your mind what it is you desire.

After you have done this, take a pad of paper and write out what you want to happen.

For example: "I, (put your name here), will get a better paying job soon." Write this statement fifteen times in a row, once a day, for as long as it takes. Usually you will start to see amazing coincidences within the first week of doing

# BECOME A SUPER-BEING

this method. Always make sure you write out what you "will" accomplish, not what you "want" to accomplish. For example, writing out "I want to get a better paying job" won't work because saying you "want" something to happen makes the statement already true. You must command yourself into a better reality by always saying that "you will" achieve your desired goal.

This technique is so simple that most people refuse to try it because it seems too easy to actually work. However, it does work for those who believe that they can master their reality.

How this method works is open to speculation. Some researchers think that our reality is made up of an infinite number of universes, each universe slightly different from the other. Our minds, or souls if you like, are skimming through these universes moment by moment. Sort of like individual frames on a reel of film. The movement of our minds through these realities creates the illusion that there is time and motion. By exercising control of our thoughts, we can "choose" which probable universes we skim through.

Some realities are more probable then others. It would take quite a bit of mind power to steer yourself into a reality where you are say President of the United States. However, every four years someone is elected President, so even the most unlikely scenarios can and do occur. Tape recorders are also very good at making your thoughts reality. You can say on the tape recorder what will happen, be it love, wealth, or health, you can influence whatever you like with your words. Put a clear suggestion of what will happen in your life on to a cassette and then replay the tape. Live that reality and you will receive that reality.

## Using Your Mental Energy

Many people still find it difficult to stop the erratic thoughts that cascade through their minds every day. There are numerous techniques that have been developed over the centuries to teach individuals methods to stem the tide of out of control thoughts.

Danilo D'Antonio, in his article *From Mind to Energy: An Oriental Meditation Primer*, details some interesting ideas on the power and control of the human mind. D'Antonio observes that we are usually so engaged with our thoughts that we don't notice they live in an "environment" which is much wider than themselves.

Like the words written in this book, thoughts seem to float on a sea, on an ocean which is very little known. Psychology doesn't help us very much because it is concerned only with the mind, considered like a group of thoughts, and it leaves out all the rest, if there is really something else to be considered. Let's attempt to gain more insight. Let's sit in a peaceful place and observe ourselves.

Immediately many thoughts come into our head. It doesn't matter. Let's wait a few more minutes. Sooner or later we notice that there is something between a thought and another one, a space, an empty space, a lack of thought if you will. If we wait a little longer, that space become larger and then we can begin to look into it. We are in a condition similar to that in which we are when we expect to perceive something.

At first we are a little strained. It is a little difficult to live such an unusual situation. We are used to having everything under control while in this case we have to put ourselves in the condition of simple observers. Slowly, however, we become familiar with this practice and feel more and more at our ease. We slide into a deeper and deeper relaxation so that we have to be careful not to fall asleep.

The immediate purpose is just staying in a condition of relaxed waking. This is the ideal condition in which to examine a subject which this time will not be something external to us but ourselves. The observer turns his attention to himself. It is the only way to get to know the inner self better. A few minutes of this exercise every day are very useful to separate us a little from our usual thoughts and it lets us enjoy more peace and balance. Since our thoughts feel observed, they stop being so tyrannical with us, come back under our control and fight no longer against us. They appear to us for that they are: a simple, partial, limited expression of our being.

Everybody knows you obtain great results only with loving daily care and so it is even in this case. If we continue observing what we are, our thoughts, our emotions, our sensations, we discover things that are more and more important. We find out that thoughts, emotions, sensations are interconnected so that they are a whole. We find that our breath itself, in its rhythm, in its depth, is strictly connected to them. The same thing happens to the little movements of our body, to our whole posture.

We discover that minor external events, the roar of a car, an insect that flies away, change our being. We find out that the same environmental situation is lived in a different way according to our interior feelings. As days go by offering us more and more experiences in those minutes we devote to ourselves, we enjoy perceptions, insights, little and great enlightenments that are a source of happiness and good humor.

Thoughts still come into our head even if with less insistence and suddenly, while we still observe us, we make one of the most beautiful discoveries of our life. Whatever thought crosses our mind, it now doesn't seem so important and absolute as before. We don't identify ourselves with every thought, on the contrary, we can even understand why that voice is arising in ourselves. We remember having heard that idea from somebody or having read it in a book or having drawn it from other preceding ideas which however have an origin external to our "EGO."

However much we strive, there is nothing that is really original and only ours. All the thoughts we have examined make us say: "I am not this thought, this thought is not mine." Suddenly we feel free from all our convictions. Opinions, ideals, judgments on which we have based our life, perhaps spoiling it a little bit, no longer appear to us as something intimate, something absolutely personal but, on the contrary, they seem to depend completely on the external world. We notice that every minor event such as a movement, a breath, a thought, has infinite causes and infinite effects. Similarly also every minor change in the environment, something that moves, temperature, moisture, lights or anything else have effects on us.

We cannot help noticing that all that exists is an infinite group of phenomena of cause and effect. Everything, such as a drop of rain, a living being, a stone, a newspaper, a car, a sneeze, an idea, everything is a cause of infinite effects and effect of infinite causes. We experience an infinite group of phenomena of causes and effects which constitutes our being. This continues uninterruptedly out of us and mix intimately with the infinite phenomena of causes and effects in the universe. We feel a deep sense of interdependence, of belonging to the whole world. We understand that this world is a unique, infinite living system where all interacts, all communicates with all, all is conscious of all.

# BECOME A SUPER-BEING

Some have called this living system God. Names ultimately mean nothing. It simply IS.

We understand more and more deeply how those choices which seemed to belong only to our mind, are in reality an expression of the universe we belong to. Our verbal expression itself, the language, we trusted blindly up to a few days ago, seems to be inadequate to express what we feel. Scientists say there is nothing but energy. Everything is energy. Everything that exists is energy. Does it makes any difference if we use the word consciousness instead of the word energy? We are electrical organisms. It doesn't take much of a scientific leap to assume that we are capable of producing and receiving radio signals that can be processed in our brain.

We can communicate with other organisms in a myriad of ways, and this allows our consciousness to design a custom reality in the following way. Imagine that your consciousness forms an aura of radio influence that is detectable to those around you. Your personal agenda would create its own beacon that would represent your inner state of being. When you come into contact with other people, their aura would either conflict, contribute, or be neutral to your aura. In that way, your aura would precede you, and would make it more likely that you would find circumstances that further your own agenda.

Since reality is both processed and created by the mind, there is a recursive nature to reality. Think of this relationship in the context of information as a fuel. It is as if our mind is the producer of the fuel that it uses to run on. We control the nature of the fuel with our thoughts and actions. External phenomena can override our own creations, but for the most part, our environment is our own. No matter what your mind or beliefs tell you, you never get more than you can handle.

If you find that you have arrived at a point in your life where a certain situation is "dropped in your lap," and you find yourself recoiling from it, relax. Take heed. You are never given anything that is beyond you, because that would be pointless. The universe has no pointless or extraneous creations. Sometimes though the universe gives you a little "cosmic kick in the pants" to push you into a direction you should be heading. Don't fight it, we need to experience life to its fullest, you can't achieve that goal by playing it nice and safe your entire life.

# BECOME A SUPER-BEING

With this new awareness comes the realization that we are all intimately connected to each other and the universe as a whole. Each one of us are projections from the Big Bang. This process is not some past event, but is timeless, continuing the process of creation infinitely. With this comes the knowledge that every single individual on this planet is already as powerful as he or she needs to be to create any reality desired, without having to hurt yourself, or anyone else, to get it. That's how powerful you are.

## Our Place In The Universe

In our past, before time-space expanded, we as spirits lived in an environment that was so easy to contend with, that out of sheer boredom we began to think of something that was daring indeed. By the infinite numbers we decided to create a new reality and the object was to live in this new reality with a new kind of body. We called it the physical reality and by means of our thoughts we created the multiverse.

Naturally we did not have the faintest idea how all this would work out, but one thing was established. It meant that all of us would have free will to participate. Once this decision was made we committed ourselves to continue this new creation until all of us were free from it in Spirit. This meant, that none of us could pull out of this commitment and leave dangling obligations toward any other spirit or participant (Karma).

We have entered into our creation in which all of us have free will. In addition, all of us take turns again and again in appearing within our self created surroundings. Our entire environment then, has been created by our thoughts. For thought is the Creator. All this means naturally, that we have been involved with our creation from the very beginning, although it is difficult to speak of beginnings since space-time are created conditions of our experiment. Thus, by means of our personal and our collective thoughts, we created the world we live in. We have been in this world for such a long time that we have completely forgotten why and how we got here in the first place and what our original intent was. Eventually however, we will all become aware, that the reality we have created consists of an energy that is a reflection of our very mind or consciousness.

# BECOME A SUPER-BEING

It is so real to us, that it fools many of our scientists. They see everything as being separate rather than intimately connected. It will be a long time before all of us understand that the environment we live in, is our own thought in physical form. The world is the manifestation of our mind, and in actuality is only virtually real. The physical universe is our mind frozen in an infinitely changing form.

We as spirits live in a vehicle or body that is composed of slowed energy, the Mind made physical. Something that is virtually real however, is an illusion. For now, we are subjected to this illusion. In lieu thereof; we are all free to celebrate the beauty of this illusionary reality. To discover the truth about our reality and master it, is a task that needs to be completed before we are free to leave this reality for good. This is what many old Masters have done and all of us, are in the evolutionary process of doing the same thing.

So in actuality we as human beings live in this physical world but we really are spirits and very few of us are aware that the entire "play" is nothing but a product of our own mind. Our mind however is not just some kind of personal property, for the energy we are, is an aspect of the universal Creator. Who in its wisdom divides itself in order to create new and daring endeavors to keep itself enchanted and cosmically occupied.

Our actions then, are the very actions of the Creator, who because of its endeavors, seems to be lost in its own play or creation. Since we are the aspects of this Creator, we really are the ones lost. Very few of us however are ready to admit this. All realities are virtual realities and the only thing that is real is the essence of the universal Creator we are aspects of.

It is a reality that is created by biochemical computers known to us as our brain and conscious mind. It is also a holographic reality, for all beings and things are holographic images or reflections of the Creator. Once you except the fact that you can actually control reality with your thoughts, then nothing is impossible. Over the years, mankind has created various forms of magic, spells, charms and incantations in an attempt to influence the conditions around them.

In truth, these forms of magic do indeed work because the practitioner unknowingly used mind power to achieve their goals. Magic is a way to focus the mind in such a way that consciousness moves through the multiverse to probabilities where the goal can occur.

# BECOME A SUPER-BEING

# BECOME A SUPER-BEING

## CHAPTER FOUR - EVERYTHING OLD IS NEW AGAIN
### Gnothei's Auton—Know Thyself
### Oracle Of Delphi

**THE** idea that there exists a power in the universe that can be controlled through special words, sacred objects or certain movements of the body, is a belief that is probably as old as mankind itself. This controlling power is what we now call magic, or to differentiate from the sleight of hand stage magicians, magick.

From the previous chapters we have learned that the ultimate energy of the universe is thought and consciousness. This energy has the ability to control where we place ourselves in the multiverse. The controlling factor is the ability to manipulate our thoughts in order to achieve our goals.

Often the human mind needs a focus to direct our thoughts and consciousness in order to change reality. This focus can be the thousands of spells, incantations and other forms of magick that have been handed down to us from past generations.

Anyone familiar with magick has undoubtedly seen the extremely complicated spells written in ancient Grimoires and other books of magick. These methods were deliberately made complicated in order to properly focus the mind. Now, however, with the realization that thoughts are the actual power behind magick, we can now use less complicated spells to achieve what is needed. This ability can also be extended to crystal/ gemstone powers, magickal and healing herbs, candle magic and others.

# BECOME A SUPER-BEING

From a religious standpoint, magick spells are a means of communicating with a deity. They are prayers to the God and Goddess, to the One, to Spirit, or whatever form the deity takes to each person. From a practical standpoint, spells are a proven way to manipulate thought energy to work for specific purposes as outlined in the particular spell. Like recipes, they are exchanged and altered to suit the taste of each person who uses them. They are colored by the personalities of the people who work them. Spells can take many forms; some spells are simply thoughts and meditations. Other magick spells, like the ones provided here, have many ingredients in them that allow the practitioner to ease into the mindset of the spell and focus energy on the desired outcome.

The magick of the spell is enhanced and supported by the physical actions taken, words spoken, herbs carried, incense burned, candles lit, and many other methods used by people to reinforce their wills. The stereotype of Witches cursing or hexing people evolved out of fear of the unknown, and the negative connotations associated with spell casting have been perpetuated by religious groups and movies depicting Witches as evil, devil worshiping, malevolent magic makers.

Spells are not necessarily "Good" or "Evil" in nature. Spells are what you make them. Don't be fooled by the name of a spell: a "Love Spell" that forces the emotion on an unwilling person is manipulative, and will surely backfire. The Karmic Rule applies: spells worked with the permission of everyone involved and for the good of all bring benefits, while spells of a manipulative nature bring the invested intent into the life of the person who sought to cause the harm.

Love spells, while seemingly harmless, can actually bend the will of the target. How would you feel if you were forced to do something against your will? You should keep this in mind before attempting manipulative magic on anyone.

## What Is A Spell?

The spell is the heart of folk magick. It is simply a ritual in which various tools are purposefully used, the goal is fully stated (in words, pictures or within the mind), and energy is moved to bring about the needed result.

## BECOME A SUPER-BEING

Spells can be as simple as reciting a short chant over a fresh rose while placing it between two pink candles in order to draw love; forming and retaining an image of the needed result in the mind; or placing a quartz crystal in a sunny window for protection purposes.

To perform effective magick three necessities must be present: The Need, the Emotion and the Knowledge. It has been said that magick was the first religion, and that if you lovingly utilize the forces of nature to cause beneficial change, you also become one of them. It is these powers that have been personified as Goddesses and Gods. Attuning with them is a spiritual experience and is the basis of all religion. Spells are the caster's will made to manifest in reality. A person's desire for something, can be a spell. Desire isn't enough often, so those that choose to learn will perform a spell to make their desire happen.

The desired event can be anything from needing cash to pay the bills to finding that special someone. Magick is usually classified as being black, white, or grey. The colors are just an easy way of remembering the distinctions, in and of themselves the colors don't mean anything. Black isn't evil, white isn't good and grey isn't somewhere in between.

White magick is magick intended to affect and improve upon one's life, black magick is magick that intends to degrade either one's own life, or another's, grey magick is magick intended to improve someone else's life. White Magick is life. It's about healing, joy and long life.

White Magick is intended for the betterment of all humans. It's also about learning to control your own mind, body, and energy. A healthy, loving person practices white magick. White magick encompasses everything, it is the balance between life and death.

There is a balancing point, describing the way things are ordered, white magick moves the balance point. Instead of being sick, you are well, instead of a world full of suffering, there is a world full of joy. Both sickness and suffering aren't removed from the person/world, they are lessened and controlled by health and joy, but can't be removed, to do so would result in the opposite of the desired effect.

Black magick is death and pain and suffering for no other reason than the fact that the caster desires it. Revenge can and often does fall into this area of magick, but revenge can be white magick as well. Magick is the art and science

# BECOME A SUPER-BEING

concerned with producing changes in the subjective reality of the operator. This means making changes in the world. These changes have to be made on purpose, and are done by using thought energy.

Practical Magick affects probability. It increases the chances that an event will happen in the desired way. There are always elements that are beyond the control of the operator, which may result in the desired goal not being achieved, but the Magick alters the odds a bit to increase the probability that it will.

For example: It may not be possible to ensure that a given toss of a coin will result in "heads up" 100% of the time, but one may be able to get it to do so more than 50% of the time.

A more practical example: One does a Magick to get money, it is not likely to just appear and flutter to the ground at your feet, more likely, you might find a job, have an old debt paid to you, find some money you had believed lost, receive a gift, perhaps even just be in the right place at the right time when a $10 bill blows down the street. Properly applied, this gives the operator all the advantage needed to interact with reality more effectively.

## What Is An Incantation?

Permeating human culture is the notion that one can influence events with magical words, prayers and mantras. Believers point to favored results, where a practitioner mutters the right words and afterwards the desired effect occurred. Much of the desired effect is brought about in the human giving the chant or his audience due to mental energy. The practitioner and his audience believe the effect will occur, and unconsciously use their mental energy to skim through the universe where the desired effect occurs. Thus if the chant was to make an ill person well, the person will announce that he or she indeed feels better and the care givers will affirm this. Since health is as much in the mind of the patient and his attendants as in the actual physical state of the patient, an observed improvement is possible.

Incantations can also be The Call, if done with a sincere wish for assistance outside of oneself. Ordinarily the practitioner and his audience are fervently desiring the outcome, and thus The Call is being given. Here something extraordinary may occur, as multiple calls have been given and all may be answered, simultaneously. Each individual in this drama may thus have a different mindset as a result of their individual conferences. They may have received new information or new insight into matters. The energy of this change within several individuals can result in extraordinary activity on the part of the group, activity that results in an outcome not previously possible.

For example, a community is suddenly plagued by rats, a local shaman uses incantations to persuade the rats to leave. Suddenly, many individuals at the same time realize that the rats are being attracted to the town's dump. Cleaning the dump gets rid of the rats. The success is attributed to the incantations, when in fact the exact words had nothing to do with the process. The words serve only as a focus for mental energy.

## Fetishes And Charms

Fetishism is the concept of a spirit entering an object, an animal, or a person. Primitive man turned many unusual things into fetishes including volcanoes, comets, pebbles, fire, holy water, trees, plants, fruits, animals, days of the week, numbers, saliva, hair, nails, skulls, umbilical cords, handicapped people, lunatics, intoxicants, poisons, bones, fireplaces, altars and temples.

Many unusual customs arose from fetishism. Friday was considered an unlucky day. Three and seven were lucky numbers, but thirteen was unlucky. When animals became fetishes, taboos on eating them evolved. When geniuses were considered fetishes, they resorted to trickery to wield power and authority over other men. Israelites believed that the spirit of God actually lived in their stone altars. Skeletal remains of saints and heroes are still regarded with superstitious awe by many.

Magical charm was credited to human flesh, tiger claws, crocodile teeth, snake venom, bones, dust of footprints, bodily secretions, effigies, black cats, wands, drums, bells, and knots. Names were esteemed so highly that ancient people each had two; their sacred name which they didn't reveal easily, and their nickname for everyday use.

# BECOME A SUPER-BEING

Moses tried to control the fetish worship of the Hebrews by forbidding them to create images. This did lessen fetish worship, but it also greatly retarded art and the enjoyment of beauty. Ironically, Moses' mandate against fetishes, became a fetish itself.

Words became fetishes, especially those words considered to be words of God. Doctrines can become fetishes, leading to bigotry, intolerance, and fanaticism. Books become fetishes when religionists believe not only that the book is true, but also that every truth is contained therein. The practice of opening a book at random while seeking advice on life decisions is fetishism too.

Totemism was a combination of social and religious observance; respect for a totem animal was believed to ensure a steady food supply for the tribe. Totems were eventually replaced by flags and other national symbols. Modern fetishes include the insignia of priests and royalty. Even public opinion has been exalted into the realm of fetishism.

Medicine men, priests, and shamans practiced public magic for the good of the whole tribe, while witches, wizards, and sorcerers were believed to have used personal magic to bring evil on enemies. The practice of using objects as charms continues today.

Go to any bingo parlor and observe the number of people who bring "lucky charms" with them as they play the game. Sports figures claim that they can't have a winning game unless they are wearing a piece of "lucky" clothing. All of our everyday lives are intertwined with the unconscious belief in lucky charms.

While sceptics scoff at the belief that an inanimate object can bring good or bad luck, the fact remains that something must be working in order for the belief to have survived over the millenniums. People will not continue doing something if it doesn't work.

Mankind has discovered that having a "special" object seems to bring about fortunate events. However, is it the object that brings the luck, or the mind of the holder affecting reality to bring about an event? Lucky charms do work. That much is certain. They work because they serve as a focus for mental energy. So in reality charms do bring about the desired effect. In essence the charm becomes one with its owner. Actually, the charm and everything else in the universe is already one with the owner, but due to the effect the material universe has on the mind, we seldom realize that we are, and always will be, one.

## BECOME A SUPER-BEING

Using Magick to help you achieve your desired goals is an excellent way to focus your amazing mental energies. It doesn't matter what kind of Magick you use, pick a form that seems best suited for you. You'll know when you find the right kind for your personal needs.

Remember that Magick doesn't have to be complex to work. Good results comes from the proper focusing of your mental energies. With this in mind, I have gathered together in this book all kinds of easy forms of Magick to assist you in finding your place in this universe. However, you must always remember not to abuse your powers. If you attempt to hurt or exploit others, it can bounce back and harm you.

# BECOME A SUPER-BEING

# BECOME A SUPER-BEING

## CHAPTER FIVE – FOLK MAGICK

*And the end of all our exploring will be to arrive where we started, and know the place for the first time.*

### Thomas Stearns Elliot

**FOLK** magick was born in an age of mystery. Thousands of years ago, nature was a strange force, points of light hung far overhead in the sky. Invisible forces ruffled hair and kicked up dust storms. Water fell from the sky. Powerful forces, inconceivable to humans, sent flashes of light from the skies, blasting trees into ashes. Women miraculously bore young. All that lived eventually died. Blood was sacred, food was sacred. Water, the Earth, plants, animals, the wind and all that existed was infused with power.

Folk magick slowly developed from these beginnings. Every group, every tribe had its own forms of ritual. Folk magick differed from structured religion and organized magick, this was the realm of personal magic, performed for personal reasons. A woman dressed a wound with a plantain leaf that she had gathered with her left hand to increase its healing properties. The fisherman rubbed his bone hooks with flowers to attract fish. Love sick teens gathered heart shaped stones and presented these to the objects of their desire.

These simple rituals continued to be used for many thousands of years, particularly in isolated areas. With the growing tide of organized religions, many of the old ways of folk magick were forgotten. Others were altered to outwardly conform to the new religions. That magick which couldn't be made to at least vaguely conform to the new religion was practiced in secret. However, folk magick had not died out completely, folk magic continued to exist.

# BECOME A SUPER-BEING

Throughout the Far, Near and Middle East, in Africa, Polynesia and Australia, in Central and South America, in rural sections of North America such as the Ozarks, in Hawaii and even in parts of Europe, folk magick still existed and was practiced. During the 1960's, folk magick saw a rebirth. The youth movement in the United States rebelled against rigid social codes and Christian ideals. Some turned to Buddhism, Zen and other Eastern teachings. Others became entranced with what little they could learn of spells, charms, herb magic, tarot cards, amulets and talismans. Countless popular books and articles appeared, revealing this once public knowledge to a new generation dissatisfied with their purely technological lives.

Today, the resurgence that began in the late 1960's has produced a generation of aware individuals. Many of these folk magickians have also become involved in channeling, psychic healing, herbal medicine, crystal consciousness, vegetarian diets, meditation and Asian teachings. Folk magick constitutes the bulk of ancient and modern magickal techniques practiced by individuals to improve their lives.

What folk magick isn't is almost as important as what it is. It isn't the "Devil's work." Is isn't "Satanism." It doesn't involve sacrifices of humans or animals. It isn't talking to spirits or calling up "demons."

It isn't dark, dangerous or evil. Folk magick isn't anti Christian or anti religion. Folk magick is pro healing and pro love. It is a tool with which people can transform their lives. When normal means fail, when all efforts have brought no results, many millions today turn to folk magick.

At the heart of folk magick is the spell. This is simply a ritual in which various tools are purposefully used, the goal is fully stated, and energy is moved to bring about the needed result. Spells are usually misunderstood by non practitioners. In popular thought, all you need to perform magick is a spell.

In folk magick, spells, words, chants, gestures with tools, are the outer form only. The real magick, the movement of energy, is within the magician. No demonic power flows to help the spell caster. Instead, the magician by correctly performing a genuine spell, builds up the power within. At the proper time this power is released to work in manifesting the spell.

Effective spells are designed to facilitate this energy. So, while "true" spells do exist, the actual magick isn't in the words or tools, it is within the folk magician. Real spells are being written every day. Old spells have no more power than new ones. Although personal power, that which resides within the magician, is the most potent force at work in folk magick, practitioners borrow freely from the spells and rituals of various cultures, using a wide variety of magical equipment.

These tools are used to help focus the mental energies and put the magician in the proper frame of mind to perform the spell. Folk magick also affects the collective unconscious, removing the filters we put upon ourselves every day. However, no matter how many times the magick is performed, it will not work unless you support the magick with action.

Magick works by using coincidence, so be alert when the conjunctions start to happen. Folk magick spells can be as simple as reciting a short chant over a fresh rose while placing it between two pink candles in order to draw love; forming and retaining an image of the needed result in the mind; or placing a quartz crystal in a sunny window for protection purposes. To perform effective magick three necessities must be present: The Need, the Emotion and the Knowledge.

## How To Choose Words Of Power

When you practice folk magick you must clearly state your need. State all dimensions of your need (enduring love, rather than just love; complete protection, rather than just physical protection; etc.). If possible, mention some of the tools that you've decided to use in the spell in your words of power or magickal rhyme. Indeed, for some spells, these words may help you to structure the entire rhyme or chant.

Use hypnotic words (those beginning with S or containing a Z) for psychic awareness, love and healing spells. Use potent, strong words for protection spells. match the words to the type of ritual you're composing.

Don't expect the words to simply flow from you. Work at it and work with them. Your psychic mind knows what you need. A good example of a simple, yet extremely effective folk magick spell is intended to bring about a personal desire, such as a love interest.

# BECOME A SUPER-BEING

*Earth and Sea, Keep harm from me.*
*Wind and Fire, Bring my desire.*

## Spells To Bind

A binding spell is the act of grasping the negative energy that is propelling a person or thing and stopping it. In a way, you are negating the unhealthy energy. The most important thing to remember when conducting a binding spell is that you must control your own violent emotions of hatred or fear. The binding spell is for protection only, not for harm. The binding itself is a very simple matter. A doll can be sewn to represent the malicious person. Fill it with earth (grave dirt if you can find it), rosemary, sage, a piece of smoky quartz and a piece of amethyst. Also enclose a piece of the person's fingernails, a lock of hair, or another personal item. Handwriting can be enclosed if you have nothing else. Photos can also be effectively used.

If your intention at any time during the ritual is to harm that person, remember that you will only bring harm upon yourself, so be very, very careful. If you can't do the ritual right away, store the doll (with the head still open) in a white cloth. During the ritual, you will sew up the head while connecting a psychic link. You then say out loud: *As this doll is bound, so too is my enemy.* Then you will proceed to sew arms & legs of the doll together. You will finish by wrapping the doll mummy fashion with a black ribbon. Bury the doll when you have completed the ritual.

A person can also be bound using mental capabilities. Placing a sample of a person's handwriting and copper tightly in an old bell jar is a way of stopping malicious gossip. When the danger is over, burn the handwriting.

## A Moonbeam Spell To Bring On Sleep

Take your pillow to a dry area beneath the moonbeams. Sprinkle a rosemary infusion around it. Work in a counterclockwise manner as you repeat, *Away from me the thoughts of day, away from me my worried ways.*

# BECOME A SUPER-BEING

Then change your direction to clockwise, altering the incantation to: *When Luna smiles through night's sky, so sleep will come to tired eyes. No more to wake, no more to roam, rest is welcome in my home.*

Repeat this last phrase as you put your head on the pillow every night. This spell is good for banishing or easing insomnia and obtaining a peaceful rest. It's best to try this spell when the Moon is just rising in the sky, especially with the Moon in Gemini or Aquarius.

## Spell For Internal Well-Being

This simple spell has been very effective in harmonizing our inner mechanisms and bringing a feeling of well being and inner peace.

1. Obtain a vial (about half a cup) of water from a steadily flowing river and put aside.

2. Light two blue candles and place at the north and south points of a circle.

3. Light two white candles and place at the east and west points of the same circle.

4. Scatter freshly picked lavender and crushed leaves of an iceberg rose evenly around the perimeter of the circle and sit within it, facing the north point.

5. Cross the arms loosely over the chest and focus your awareness on the breath entering your body and slowly spreading through it.

6. Return your focus slowly to your environment and extinguish the candles using the river water, kneeling before each as you do so, in the order north west east south.

## A Simple Spell For Healing

This spell is a small healing spell, and will usually only work on minor muscle soreness, depending on how much energy you gather and your concentration.

It could be integrated into a more complete rite or added to if you want to improve it. It is really very simple, take a hot bath on the night of the first full

# BECOME A SUPER-BEING

moon of the month. Afterwards you should recite this spell five times while concentrating on the moon: *My aches and pains are drawn away.* You should feel better in the morning.

## Spells For Protection

To protect an object, trace a pentagram over the object with your first and middle finger. Visualize that you're leaving a purple flame where you trace and say: *With this pentagram I lay Protection here both night and day And for he who should not touch Let his fingers burn and twitch I now invoke the rule of three So it shall be.*

Here is a simple spell to protect an object. Again, trace a pentagram over the object that you wish to protect while saying: *With this pentagram Protection I lay To guard this object Both night and day And for him who should not touch May his body shiver and quake This I will So it will be.*

Another spell for protection. Sit or stand before any fire. Look into the flames (or flame, if using a candle). Visualize the fire bathing you with glowing, protective light. The fire creates a flaming, shimmering sphere around you. If you wish, say the following or similar words: *Craft the spell in the fire, Craft it well, Weave it higher. Weave it now of shining flame, None shall come to hurt or maim. None shall pass this fiery wall, None shall pass, no, none at all.*

Repeat this simple yet effective ritual everyday when in need.

## Removing A Jinx Using An Egg

For many years the ancient Voodoo priests have used the power of eggs to help combat the power of evil spells and bad luck. They believe that the egg possesses strong magical powers and in the right hands can cause bad luck or good luck depending on the will of the practitioner. If you are plagued by evil spells and bad luck, then do this powerful ancient Voodoo egg spell to help you remove any negative conditions from your life.

1. You must purchase a brown fresh egg before noon of that day. Make sure that you start this when the moon is waning. It is very important that this egg be

## BECOME A SUPER-BEING

fresh. Place this egg in a brown bag and tie the neck of the bag with a black cloth string. Place this bag under your bed.

2. Each night before retiring to bed, you must open this bag and take the egg out and rub it all over your body. When done, put the egg back into the bag, take a deep breath and blow three times into the bag. When you are blowing into the bag, you must imagine that all the bad luck is leaving your body, via your breath. When done, place the bag back under your bed. Do this for nine days. At the end of nine days, take the bag with the egg and dispose of it outside your home. There are several ways to do this. Either take the bag and bury it completely. Or, burn it with a wooden match, until the bag is entirely consumed.

3. Note: Each time that you blow into the bag, you must immediately tie it back up. If by the end of seven days you notice that your bag is moving on its own, stop, and dispose of the bag immediately.

4. DO NOT LOOK INTO THE BAG. Make sure that the bag is secure. We are not responsible for any misuse, or actions that may result from the use of this powerful spell. Do not play with this. Only do this if you are serious about destroying the bad luck in your life.

# BECOME A SUPER-BEING

# BECOME A SUPER-BEING

### CHAPTER SIX – LOVE AND MONEY

*In the mind of every thinking person there is set aside a special room, a museum of wonders. Every time we enter that museum we find our attention gripped by marvel number one, this strange Universe, in which we live and move and have our being.*

### John A. Wheeler

**MANY** who are new to magick seem to be in quite a hurry to find and use magick spells. To simply take a spell from someone's book of shadows, collect the ingredients, and go through the motions as if it were a recipe in a cookbook is not the way to go about it.

Let's say you are going to send someone special a greeting card. Instead of buying one, you decide to make your own. You have the supplies or "tools" to make the card, but everything in it is created by you. You have to spend time thinking about what you want it to say, what colors you want to use etc.

The finished card is a personal extension of you. Your energy, focus, will, visualization and intent are all in that card. And although this may seem like an overly simplistic example, those very same things are all necessary in performing magick. It comes back to the "you receive from it exactly what you put into it" principle.

To borrow aspects from other spells is fine, but remember that the spell itself was created specifically for the use of the person who designed it. For example: you may wish to perform a spell to protect your home, keep in mind that it is your home. No two people see or experience anything in the exact same way, thus, the protection spell you use should reflect your individual desire of protection. Not someone else's.

# BECOME A SUPER-BEING

Numerous people are first attracted to magick in the attempt to gain either love or money. These two desires are what seems to motivate most of us when we attempt to focus our mental energies to influence reality. There have been countless spells developed over the years to bring forth wealth and romance. As long as these spells are used in ways that won't harm or exploit others, then they can be very effective for the practitioner.

### Love Spells

This is a love spell that has been proven to work. You only need a few household supplies: A small pot, basil seeds, rich soil. Sow the seeds in a small pot thinking loving thoughts about your love. Put the pot in a warm place and water them frequently. Keep them in a warm safe place. As the basil starts to grow, visualize the object of your desire and the feelings you want him or her to feel. Sooner or later the person will start to show feelings for you and the spell has worked.

### To Attract Love

This is an incantation to attract love, recite this once a day while thinking about the person you desire:

***Be silent, Be Still Resonate at will. Resonate within yourself Feel the energy Feel the wealth. Crystal heart Love's mark Radiant to all. Color spectrum Divine light Echoing its call. Trusting now Flying wide Reaching out within. Listen close Ignore no more For now it is time to begin.***

### To Gain Love

Create or find a charred stick. You will also need a few dried rose petals and a piece of paper.

Using the charred part of the stick as you would a pencil, draw two interlinked hearts on paper as you visualize yourself enjoying a satisfying relationship.

# BECOME A SUPER-BEING

Draw with power. Hold the rose petals in your hand and send fiery, loving energies into them. Sprinkle the petals over the linked hearts. Do this with power.

Wrap the package around the petals. Still visualizing, throw the package into a fire. (Or, light it in the flame of a red candle & throw into a heat proof container.)

As it burns, the power is released.

### To Attract A Lover

This is when you have a lover but he or she is not as attentive as you wish they would be. Sit before a dying fire and gaze into it, clearing your mind of all but thoughts of your lover. Have a small basket of laurel leaves between your knees. Keeping your gaze fixed on the fire, dip your left hand into the basket, take out a handful of leaves, and toss them onto the fire. As they burst into flames, chant out loud the following:

***Laurel leaves that burn in the fire, Draw unto me my heart's desire.***

Wait until the flames have died down, then repeat the action. Do it a third time. Within 24 hours your lover will come to visit you. If this spell doesn't work after a third time try this chant.

***Lover come to me I hereby call, Do it before the new moon falls.***

### To Make Yourself Known To Another

If you love another and they don't seem to notice, then this can bring you to their attention. You need to find their footprints in the earth. You then dig up this footprint (more correctly, the earth in which it is impressed). Take the earth to the nearest willow tree and, making a hole in the ground at its base, put the footprint earth into the hole, filling it over with the original dirt. As you are burying the footprint this way, say: Many earths on earth there be, I make my love know unto thee. For He is the flower and I the stem; He the cock and I the hen. Grow, grow willow tree! Sorrow not for the likes of me.

# BECOME A SUPER-BEING

From then on you will find that the person you yearn for will indeed start to notice you. Where it goes from there, of course, is up to you.

### Simple Love Spells For Teens

To gain the love of someone: On a night of the full moon, walk to a spot beneath your beloved's bedroom window, and whisper his/her name three times to the night wind.

### Ozark love spell

Need a little help capturing the heart of the one you love? Try one of the love spells used by young people from past generations: Want to know if your love loves you? Find a daisy. As you pluck each petal from the flower, say alternately, "he/she loves me; he/she loves me not." Whatever you say as you pluck the last petal is supposed to be the truth.

Lettuce is said to be a powerful aphrodisiac, so be sure to prepare a salad for your true love. In Greek mythology, Venus laid the body of her lover on a bed of lettuce; and Juno, the wife of Jupiter, conceived Hebe after eating lettuce. Guys, if you're serious about your girl, present her with a token of three ears of wheat.

Quince was held in great esteem by the Greeks and Romans and symbolized love, fertility, and temptation. Newly married couples often shared the fruit as a symbol of their love. It is said that if you dream of quince, you'll have a very successful love life.

Do you want to know what your future husband will look like? Take a burning candle and a red apple into a dark room a few minutes before midnight on Halloween. Stand in front of a mirror and cut the apple into small pieces. Throw one piece over your right shoulder, and eat the rest of the pieces while you comb your hair. Never look behind you and when the clock strikes midnight, your future husband's face will appear in the mirror. Another way to receive a vision of

# BECOME A SUPER-BEING

your future husband is to make a "Dumb Cake" using eggs, flour, salt, and water on St. Agnes Eve (January 21). Fast all day, and eat the cake at midnight while saying the following rhyme:

***Sweet Agnes work thy fast, If ever I be to marry a man, Or ever a man to marry me, I hope him this night to see.***

If it works, an apparition of your future husband should appear to you.

Do you seek eternal beauty and youth? Get up at dawn on May Day and roll naked in the dew. Guys, if your lady love gives you a sprig of Thyme whenever you leave her, she just want you to remember her while you're away. This practice comes from the Middle Ages, when young women gave their knights gifts of thyme and scarves embroidered with designs of thyme when they embarked on long crusades. The symbolism meant "loving remembrance."

Rosemary is the emblem of remembrance and fidelity. Brides used to give bunches of it to the groom, and it was usually incorporated into the bridal wreath. A bridesmaid would often plant a sprig from the wedding bouquet into the new bride's garden to provide rosemary for future daughters.

Unsure if your lover is faithful? Lay some apple seeds on a fireplace grate and say these words:

***If you love me, bounce and fly, If you hate me, lie and die.***

If the seeds crackle and burn noisily, your lover is faithful. However, if he or she is not, the apple seeds will quietly burn away.

### The Lemon Of Love

To find if the one you love will become your spouse, do the following. In the morning, as soon as you arise, peel a small lemon. Keep two equal pieces of the peel, each about the size of a half dollar. Place the pieces with the insides together and the peel sides out, and put them in your right hand pocket or in your purse. Leave them there all day.

# BECOME A SUPER-BEING

At night, when you undress for bed, take the peel from your pocket or purse and rub the legs of the bed with it. Then place both pieces of the peel under your pillow and lay down to sleep. If you dream of your love, then you will surely marry him/her.

### Gypsy-Witch Love Potion

(To be performed during the time of the waxing Moon on a Friday, on St. Agnes's Eve, or St. Valentine's Day, when the Moon is in Taurus or Libra). Gather together a teaspoon of crushed dried basil, a teaspoon of dried fennel, a teaspoon of dried European vervain, three pinches of ground nutmeg and a quarter of a cup of red wine and cast a circle on the appropriate day. Put the ingredients in a cauldron or pot and mix them up together. Heat the cauldron over a fire and light a pink candle anointed with rose oil. Concentrate on the object of your affection while brewing the potion and incant:

*Candle light, warm and bright, Ignite the flames of love tonight. Let my soul mate's love Burn strong for me.*

Boil the potion for three minutes before removing the cauldron from the fire to let it cool. Then strain it into a cup, add honey, and drink. Or, you may drink half of the potion and let your beloved drink the other half. Remember, using force will not work. A spell cast on a unwilling subject could bounce back at the spell-caster and cause bad luck and misfortune.

### Voodoo Love Spell

One of the most powerful voodoo spells that you can do to help bring true love into your life is called the Peacock Lover Spell. This is what you must do.

Take a sheet of parchment paper and write the name of the person that you want to fall in love with you 13 times. Place this under your pillow with the Peacock feather and call the name of the person you want to be with 13 times. Do this for three nights.

On the fourth night light some incense and then take a bath and sit in the bath water for 13 minutes concentrating on the person that you want to be with.

# BECOME A SUPER-BEING

That night you will have a dream of this person and in this dream you will have the power to control the outcome of this dream. Whatever you do in this dream with this person will determine the result that you will have.

It is best to make sure that at some point in this dream that you have a sexual experience with this person. When you wake up, hide the paper somewhere in your bedroom and make sure that the person that you want finds the feather in their house, or job. This can be done by mailing this to them with no returned address, or you can secretly place it somewhere where they can find it on their job. However you do it, make very sure that they are the first one to touch this feather.

### To Gain Love

You need two pink candles and one magenta candle. Light the two pink candles and say:

*One to seek him, one to find him. One to bring him, one to bind him. Heart to heart, Forever one. So say I, this spell is done. Light the magenta candle to speed the spell on its way.*

### To Communicate With Others

Write a letter to a distant friend as if you were going to mail it. Next, light a blazing hot fire and throw the letter into it, firmly visualizing the person's face. You should receive a reply within a week.

### A Basic Love Spell

Take three cords or strings of various, pleasing pastel colors perhaps pink, red, and green. Braid them tightly together. Firmly tie a knot near one end of the braid, thinking of your need for love.

Next, tie another knot, and another, until you have tied seven knots. Wear or carry the cord with you until you find your love. After that, keep the cord in a safe place, or give to one of the elements burn and scatter the ashes in the ocean or in a stream.

# BECOME A SUPER-BEING

### To Encourage Romance

Melt wax from a red candle and let it cool only until it is still malleable. Place it in a bowl while you take three of the following herbs: Rose, dill, daisy, hibiscus, licorice, rosemary, basil, ginger, thyme, vanilla, geranium, juniper.

Mix the herbs, concentrating on your need for love. Knead the wax, adding a pinch of the herb mixture every few seconds until the wax is full of herbs. Form the wax into a heart. Wrap it in pink cloth and hang it from your bed.

### Herbal Charm to Attract Love

Fill a circle of rose or red colored cloth with any of the following: Acacia, rose, myrtle, jasmine, or lavender petals, in combination or singly. Add to this a red felt heart and copper coin or ring.

As you fill the bundle with your chosen items, visualize the type of lover you are looking for. Tie the cloth with blue thread or ribbon, in seven knots. As you tie the knots you may chant an incantation such as:

*Seven knots I tie above, Seven knots for me and love.*

### Apple Peel Spell

Peel an apple, keeping the entire peel in one long thin strip. Then throw the peeling over your left shoulder. If it stays in one piece it will reveal the initial of your one true love.

After finding the initial of your love, if you cut the apple in half and count the seeds, it will foretell how many children you will have from the union.

### To Spice Up Your Romance

Sprinkle orris powder between the sheets. Add a few drops of patchouli or musk oil to the final rinse when washing your sheets. Burn red candles in the room (red being the color of passion and energy).

# BECOME A SUPER-BEING

### Improve Your Sex Life

Dried Dragon's Blood resin beneath the bed or a branch from a fir tree suspended from the head board will help spice up your sex life if it's lagging.

### Are You Meant For Each Other?

If you are not sure whether you and your mate are meant for each other, and you are willing to forfeit the relationship should this not be the case, do this love spell. Take two silver dollars. Two pennies will also do. Toss them into the air reciting:

*May we each go to our own true love.*

Do not do this spell unless you only want to be with a true love and so are willing to forfeit your present relationship should it not represent your true love. Should the coins land far apart, do not take this as a sign that you will separate. Your true loves should reveal themselves within a month.

### Unlucky Days For Love

According to the Gypsies, the following days are considered to be unlucky for Love. Don't start a relationship, get married, etc on these dates: January 1, 2, 6, 14, 27 February 1, 17, 19 March 11, 26 April 10, 27, 28 May 11, 12 June 19 July 18, 21 August 2, 26, 27 September 10, 18 October 6 November 6, 17 December 5, 14, 23

### How To Rid Yourself Of An Unwanted Lover

This is an ideal spell for people who are bothered by a persistent suitor or stalker. This spell should be done during the waning cycle of the Moon, that is, after the Full Moon and before the New Moon. Have a roaring fire going, then go outside and pick up two handfuls of dry vervain leaves (you can place them on the ground ahead of time, if necessary.) As you pick them up, shout out the name of the one you wish to be rid of. Turn and go into the house (or cross to the fire if this is all done out in the open) and fling leaves onto the fire with the words:

# BECOME A SUPER-BEING

*Here is my pain; Take it and soar. Depart from me now and offend me no more.*

Do this for three nights. You will hear no more from your unwanted lover.

## Money Magic

Trying to obtain material wealth is probably the second most popular use of spells next to love magick. Using spells to obtain money seems to work better when used for a true need, rather than for greed. For example, if you are having trouble meeting your monthly bills, money spells might help. However, if you are performing this spell because you just want to go out on a spending spree, your results may not be as successful.

When casting a spell to obtain money, it is imperative that you state somewhere in your chant that no harm shall come to any through the working of your spell. I have heard of several cases of people doing a ritual to obtain money, and then obtaining that money through an insurance policy because a favorite relative died an untimely death, or because they were involved in a serious automobile accident. Be careful what you wish for, you just might get it.

Before you begin to try any spell, think if what you wish is what you really want. When you make a spell, you should not try other spells for at least two weeks. If your wish comes true in less than two weeks, go ahead and try some other spells. When you feel that nothing is happening after you tried a spell, redo the spell 7 days (or later) after the day you tried the first time or last.

Making a spell does take energy from you spiritually, and you may need to rest after you try it. The important thing is that you make every possible effort to make your wish come true. Focus your attention onto your wish. Don't just depend on the spells to work on their own. Without your making efforts, spells won't be able to accomplish their missions.

# BECOME A SUPER-BEING

## Eliminate Poverty

To keep poverty away you need to get some: Sugar, salt, rice, an open safety pin. Based on a New Orleans voodoo formula, this spell will insure that you always have the staples in life. Fill a bowl with equal parts sugar, salt, and rice. Place an open safety pin in its center. Keep the bowl out in the open to scare away poverty.

## The Magic Money Chant

Please bless _____ with new prosperity and a sudden increase of abundance. Starting now, and continuing for the rest of _____ days, let a golden river of glittering money pour into _____ life, filling it with sunshine, happiness and contentment. Let everything _____ touches turn to gold, and every enterprise or endeavor in which _____ is involved bring _____ the maximum rewards, without risk or loss of any kind. Shower _____ with _____'s every want, for as long as _____ remains worthy. Let life make known unto _____ it's joys, it's happiness. Let life reveal to _____ the fruits of our faith, the ripe, rich succulent fruits of good fortune. Let it proffer to _____ these offerings, for _____ to pluck to _____'s heart's delight to taste and savor endlessly for the rest of _____'s days. For _____ is a good person, and will conduct _____ self in a manner worthy of the good fortune with which _____ is blessed sharing and helping others along the way. Let _____ therefore know, now, any and all luxuries in which _____ envisions for _____ is a true believer in the Maxim, "If there is any good I can do my fellow (hu)man, let me do it now, for I shall pass this way but once. Blessed Be. Repeat this chant once a day, usually when you first get out of bed.

## To Obtain Money

An extremely simple yet effective spell for obtaining fast money when needed is the following: On a Friday during the Waxing Moon anoint a green candle with an appropriate money drawing oil, such as Patchouli, Jasmine, or Cinnamon. Take the candle and place in a holder. Place a brand new shiny penny in front of the holder, and then surround the holder with three green aventurine gemstones. Repeat the following chant 3 times:

# BECOME A SUPER-BEING

***Money, money come to me, $100 is what I need. With harm to none and help to many, multiply now this shiny penny!***

Now light your candle and gaze into its flame, strongly visualizing the needed money coming to you. Continue with this visualization for as long as possible. After the candle has burned down completely, bury any remaining wax on your property and carry the penny with you to reinforce your magickal intention.

**A Silver Spell**

Situate a small bowl of any material in a place of prominence in your home, somewhere you pass by every day. Each day for seven days put one dime in the bowl. Next, obtain a green candle, any shape or kind.

Before you begin, fix in your mind the idea that you are a prosperous person. See money as being no problem. Imagine money coming to you, as you need it. Place the bowl of dimes, the candle and a candle holder on a flat surface. Hold the candles in your hands and feel the power of money. Feel the avenues that open to you when you have it. Sense the energy within money which we as human beings have given to it.

Place the candle in the holder. Pour the seven dimes into your left hand. You will create a circle surrounding the candles with the dimes. Place the first dime directly before the candle. As you place it say these or similar words:

***Money flow, money shine, Money grow, Money mine.***

Repeat this six more times until you've created a circle around the candle with seven gleaming dimes. As you say the words and place the dimes, know that you're not just reciting and fooling around with pieces of metal. You're working with power, that which we've given money as well as that which is within yourself. Words have energy, as does the breathe on which they ride.

When you've completed this, light the candle. Strike a match and touch its tip to the wick. As it puts up the fire, sputters, to a shining flames, see money burning these. See the power of money flowing out from the seven dimes up to the candle's flames and then out to the atmosphere.

# BECOME A SUPER-BEING

Blow out the match and settle down before the glowing candle and money. Sense the feeling of money in your life. Visualize a life with money to spare, a life in which bills are quickly paid and money will never again be a problem.

See yourself wisely spending money, investing it for your future needs. See money as an unavoidable and beautiful aspect of your life.

Kill off any thoughts of debt, of taxes, of doubt that you can achieve this change. Simply see what will be. See what is to be real.

After ten minutes or so, leave the area. Let the candle burn itself out in the holder.

Afterward, collect the dimes, place them back in the bowl, and "feed" it a few coins every day from then on. Money will come to you.

## Buckeye Nuts To Attract Wealth

The Buckeye nut has long been carried by men in the mid-western states as a good luck charm. The "doctrine of signatures," the magical belief that items from nature reveal their purpose or usefulness by their shape, color, or markings, may be what gives buckeyes their status as good luck charms among men, for by "luck," they mean good fortune in sexual and financial matters.

In addition to increasing the bearer's money power, the buckeye is thought by many people in the eastern and southern United States to be a sure preventive of rheumatism or headache. Identical beliefs were recorded in Germany and the Netherlands during the early 19th century, but there the preventive power was attributed to the buckeye's European relative, the horse chestnut. It is probable that European immigrants transferred the horse chestnut's magical ability to the buckeye when they settled in America. In the African American voodoo tradition, a buckeye in the pocket is reputed to increase one's supply of pocket money and to increase a gambler's luck.

## A Magick Wish List

To make a magick wish list, sit back for about fifteen minutes and think about the material things you need. Really evaluate them, discarding what is not truly necessary, selecting only those that you must have. Then write out a spell,

# BECOME A SUPER-BEING

asking in the name of a higher source for the items you need. List them and read the list over out loud. By reciting the list you are charging your intentions with vocal vibrations and the projection is fortified with magickal energy. Burn the list or carry it with you or keep it in a safe place that only you know about.

## Simple Candle Spell To Bring Money

You will need one green candle, a candle holder and a lighter. If you really want to be in sync with natural energies, do this visualization during the waxing moon i.e. during the two weeks when the Moon is increasing in light, from New to Full.

Close your eyes and breathe slowly, deeply and rhythmically until you feel completely relaxed. Imagine yourself surrounded by white light, enclosed in a bright bubble of energy or otherwise protected from harm. If it makes you more comfortable call upon the Creator, your personal guardian angel, spirit guide, or patron saint to be with you in this work.

Begin to visualize money flowing into your life. You don't have to imagine how this is going to happen. In your mind's eye see dollar bills or silver dollars or whatever signifies money to you being blown towards you from above and from all directions. What does it feel like to have this money, to have the ability to pay all your bills or the freedom to buy what you most want? Try to both mentally picture this as clearly as you can and feel it emotionally.

Now pick up the candle and hold it tightly in your hands until you feel your pulse throbbing beneath your fingers. Your energy and the prosperous energies of the universe symbolized by the green candle are merging together. You are becoming a prosperity magnet. Affirm your desire (to yourself or out loud). For example:

***Money streams continuously into my life, with harm towards none.***

Continue visualizing and chanting as you place the candle in the holder and light it. Cup your hands around the flame, feeling it's warmth and energy. Put the candle in a safe place and let it burn down naturally.

# BECOME A SUPER-BEING

## Magnetic Lodestone To Attract Wealth

A lodestone is a naturally magnetic piece of iron. Lodestones can be bought from rock shops or ordered through the mail from science catalogs. The lodestone has been held in high regard by the Ancient Romans, Chinese and other people as a powerful amulet and good luck charm. Probably because the magnetic influence of this stone was supposed to attract power, favors and gifts.

It is said that the ancient Romans believed that lodestone kept husband and wife faithful, and made their love secure.

The following voodoo lodestone spell can be used for drawing anything you want, whether it is money, romance, sex, marriage, a new car, business success, a child, a job, or the return of a lost lover.

You need one large lodestone, a china plate, a packet of iron filings that have been magnetized, and a piece of parchment. Write your wish on the parchment, being as specific as possible about your wants. If you have a picture of what you desire (whether a person or an object), add that as well. If your desire is for more money, add some coins or bills to your written wish.

Place the wishing paper, the picture, and any bills on the plate and put the lodestone on top. Pray over the lodestone, stating your wish clearly, and then feed the lodestone with a pinch of iron filings. The idea is to get the lodestone to understand your wish and to work on your behalf, drawing the desire toward you. When you have finished praying, put the plate and everything on it away where no one will see it. Every day take out the plate with the lodestone and papers, pray over it, and feed the lodestone with iron filings, stating your wish clearly.

When your wish comes true, thank the lodestone and bury it with all the papers, still on the plate, somewhere in your yard. The place you bury your lodestone is very important. The natural forces of the earth will carry away any residual magick that may still be contained within. Make sure that no one disturbs the lodestone for at least one year after its burial. After one year's time, the stone will be clean.

## Lucky Charms Invoking St. Martin

There are two Saint Martin's in the Catholic religion; the recently canonized Saint Martin de Porres and the older Saint Martin of Tours. The latter,

# BECOME A SUPER-BEING

known in Latin America as San Martin Caballero, "Saint Martin the Horse rider," is the one most frequently encountered in luck charms.

Born in Hungary during the late Roman empire, he was pressed into service in the Roman army, where he became a centurion. One day, while riding his horse, he chanced upon a near naked beggar and cut his cloak in half to give the poor man a covering. That night he had a dream in which the beggar appeared to him as Jesus, so he quit the army and became a monk in Italy. He was later promoted to the rank of Bishop of Tours (in France) but always lived a simple life and gave a great deal to charity. Thus San Martin is used as a lucky charm by the poor, and by those who hope strangers will aid them.

In Mexico, San Martin Caballero is especially popular among shop keepers, who rely on the kindness of passing strangers for their livelihood, and among truck drivers, who see in his horsemanship a parallel to their own manner of earning a living. Because the horse he rides is associated with the lucky horseshoe, he is also a favorite saint among gamblers.

In Cuba, some Santeros identify him with the orisha Ellegua, probably because the latter is associated with crossroads and thus with travel.

## Magick Words To Draw Money

These words were believed to draw money when repeated out loud several times during the day. You can repeat each word by itself, or several at once to increase the power:

*Trinka, Kabai, Mieshur, Durla, Bhusek, Nicople, Jshnre, Yohbhe.*

## Business Success Oil

To make an anointing oil to bring business success. You will need: 6 drops Bergamot (Mint Bouquet) oil, 2 drops Basil oil, 2 drops Patchouli oil, 1 pinch of ground Cinnamon (herb, not oil), One half ounce base oil (apricot kernel, jojoba, grapeseed, even olive oil).

This is a very simple recipe, which has a multitude of uses, including: Anointing candles for business prosperity rituals. Anointing of hands. Combine with bath salts for prosperity ritual baths. Add to loose money drawing incense

# BECOME A SUPER-BEING

blends to increase its potency. Anointing of talismans and charms. Anoint the cash register, business cards, or the front door of a place of business to increase cash flow.

Keep in mind that for calling magick, such as money, love, health, luck or anything that brings something to you, it is best to perform the spells during the waxing moon (first quarter) to the full moon.

When you use folk magick to bring something to yourself, make sure it is something you really need out of life. Don't just start calling for useless material goods.

The universe works by taking the path of least resistance. That means the universe will place you into the nearest reality that conforms to your wishes. You may not receive your desires exactly the way you wanted them. I have heard stories of people who used magick spells for money, only to have their house burn down. The money then came from the insurance settlement.

# BECOME A SUPER-BEING

# BECOME A SUPER-BEING

### CHAPTER SEVEN – CANDLE MAGIC

*The true voyage of discovery lies not in seeking new landscapes, but in having new eyes.*

### Douglas Monroe: The 21 Lessons of Merlyn

**ONE** of the most popular and easiest forms of folk magick is candle burning. Its popularity is due to the fact that candle magick is relatively easy to perform, and employs little ritual and few ceremonial artifacts. The theatrical props of candle magick can be purchased at any department store and its rituals can be practiced in any quiet room of the house.

Most of us have experienced candle magick on our birthdays, blowing out the candles on our birthday cakes and making a wish is pure candle magick. This childhood custom is based on the three magickal principles of concentration, will power and visualization. In simple terms, the child who wants his wish to come true has to concentrate (blow out the candles), visualize the end result (make a wish) and hope that it will come true( will power).

The size and shape of the candles you use isn't important, although ornate, extra large, or unusually shaped candles will not be suitable. The reason being is that such candles may create distractions when the practitioner wants to concentrate on the important work in hand. Most candle-users prefer to use candles of standard or uniform size if possible. Those which are sold in different colors for home use are perfect for candle magick.

Candles used for any type of magickal invocation should be pristine. Under no circumstances use a candle which has already adorned a dinner table or been used as a bedroom candle or nightlight. The reason is that vibrations picked up

# BECOME A SUPER-BEING

by secondhand materials or equipment may disturb your workings and negate their effectiveness.

Some candle-users who are artistically inclined prefer to make their own candles for magickal use. This is a very practical exercise because not only does it impregnate the candle with your own personal vibrations, but the mere act of making your own candle is magickally potent. Craft shops which sell candle making supplies can also provide do it yourself books explaining the technicalities of the art to the beginner.

Once you have purchased or made your ritual candle, it has to be oiled or "dressed" before burning. Fragrance is an extremely useful tool. It "sets the mood" for your ritual and goes a long way in bringing about your desired magickal intention.

The purpose of dressing the candle is to establish a psychic link between it and the magician through a primal sensory experience. By physically touching the candle during the dressing procedure, you are charging it with your own personal vibrations and also concentrating the desire of your will directly into the wax. The candle will become an extension of the magician's mental power and life energy.

When you dress a candle for magickal use, imagine that it is a psychic magnet with a north and a south pole. Rub the oil into the candle beginning at the top or north end and work downwards to the half way point. Always brush in the same direction downwards. This process is then repeated by beginning at the bottom or south end and working up to the middle.

The best type of oils to use for dressing candles are natural ones which can be obtained quite easily. Some occult suppliers will provide candle magic oils with exotic names. If the practitioner does not want to use these, he can select suitable oils or perfumes from his own sources. The oil soluble perfumes sold by craft shops for inclusion in homemade candles can be used.

There are any number of popular oils that are commonly used in magick. Some have a long history of use due to their commonly accepted magickal attributes. Don't be afraid to experiment with different fragrances from oils and incense. Your personal involvement in choosing the right oils is what is important to achieve the proper results.

Here is a brief list to get you started.

# *BECOME A SUPER-BEING*

## Popular Fragrances For Candle Magic

- **Amber:** love, comfort, happiness, and healing.

- **Apple Blossom:** happiness, love, friendship.

- **Bayberry:** protection, wishes, prosperity, happiness, control.

- **Benzoin:** astral projection, purification.

- **Bergamot:** money attraction, prosperity, uplifting of spirits, protection.

- **Carnation:** protection, strength, healing, love, lust.

- **Cedarwood:** healing, purification, unhexing, protection, money attraction.

- **Cinnamon:** purification, stimulation, wealth, business success.

- **Clove:** pain relief, intellectual stimulation, divination, psychic awareness.

- **Dragon's Blood:** useful in adding power to any other oil, increases potency of spells and rituals, protection, courage, hex breaking, exorcism, love.

- **Frankincense:** spirituality, astral strength, protection, consecration, courage.

## BECOME A SUPER-BEING

- **Ginger:** wealth and riches, energizing, lust, love, magickal power.

- **Honeysuckle:** money, psychic powers, happiness, friendship, healing.

- **Jasmine:** love, money, dreams, fantasy, purification, wisdom, skills.

- **Juniper:** calming, protection, healing, happiness, good luck, spiritual exorcism.

- **Lemon:** healing, love, purification.

- **Lilac:** soothing, warding off, exorcism.

- **Musk:** aphrodisiac, prosperity, inner truth, courage, spirituality, purification.

- **Myrrh:** spirituality, hex breaking, meditation, healing, consecration.

- **Orange:** divination, love, luck, money attraction, healing abilities, psychic powers.

- **Patchouli:** growth, love, mastery, warm and sensual.

- **Peppermint:** energy, mental stimulant, exorcism, healing.

- **Pine:** grounding, strength, cleansing, exorcism, healing.

# BECOME A SUPER-BEING

- **Rose:** love, house blessing, fertility, healing.

- **Rosemary:** remembrance, energy, exorcism, healing

- **Sage:** wisdom, clarity, purification, exorcism

- **Sandalwood:** spirituality, healing, protection, astral projection.

- **Strawberry:** love, luck.

- **Vanilla:** lust, mental powers.

- **Violet:** wisdom, luck, love, protection, healing.

- **Yarrow:** courage, exorcism, psychic abilities. Basic Candle Magic

Basic candle magick deals only with two colors, white and black. Envision the white candle as the waxing to full moon and the black candle as the waning to new moon. For any calling purposes, use the white candle. For any banishing purposes, use the black candle.

Over the years the use of colored candles has gained in popularity. However, purists of folk candle magick are insistent that the use of colored candles are simply not necessary. There is also debate on whether or not colored candles serve more as a distraction rather than help the magick. Nevertheless, the use of colored candles is widely established. Each color supposedly has its own magickal significance. Candles can be colored in accordance with the following magical uses:

# BECOME A SUPER-BEING

## Colors

- **Blue:** inspiration, occult wisdom, protection and devotion.

- **Gold:** wealth, fortune, solar energy.

- **Green:** fertility, abundance, healing, good luck and harmony.

- **Orange:** ambition, career matters and the law.

- **Pink:** love affection and romance.

- **Purple:** material wealth, psychic ability, spiritual power and idealism.

- **Red:** health, energy, strength, courage, sexual potency.

- **Silver:** clairvoyance, inspiration, astral energy and intuition.

- **White:** spiritual growth, mental and physical healing.

- **Yellow:** intellectualism, imagination, memory and creativity.

The use of colored candles for folk magick is a excellent way to invoke the hidden energies. For example, if you wanted to use candle magic for healing, you would select a red candle to burn. To pass an exam, burn a yellow candle, to gain esoteric knowledge burn a blue candle or for material gain, burn a purple one.

The colors you use can also have a deeper personal significance. This is encouraged since a more intimate connection with the candles will always achieve better results. Feel free to experiment with different colors. Always

# BECOME A SUPER-BEING

remember to write down the types of success you have with different colors. That way, when you are trying to achieve a certain goal, you can go back and check your notes.

## Candle Magic Methods

The simplest form of candle magic is to write down the objective of your ritual on a virgin piece of paper. You can also use color paper which matches the color of the candle. Write your petition on the paper. As you write down what you want to accomplish through candle magic, a new job, healing for a friend, a change of residence, a new love affair, visualize your dream coming true.

Visualize the circumstances under which you might be offered a new job, imagine your employer telling you that your salary has been increased or conjure up a vision of your perfect love partner.

When you have completed writing down your petition, carefully fold up the paper in a deliberately slow fashion. Place the end of the folded paper in the candle flame and set light to it. As you do this concentrate once more on what you want from life. When you have completed your ritual, allow the candle to have completely burned away. You do not need to stay with the candle after the ritual, but make sure that is safe and that hot wax will not cause damage or fire.

Never reuse a candle which has been lit in any magickal ritual. A candle should only be used in one ritual and then allowed to burn away or be disposed of afterwards.

A note here about putting out candles, do not blow out a candle. Snuff it out. The only time you would blow out a magickal candle is when you need an emergency stop. Finalizing the energy in such a way will cause a psychic backlash, so be prepared.

Now that you are ready to try your first candle magick spell, make sure you have everything you need to insure a successful invocation. Before performing any magick be sure that you have the consent of the person you are doing magick for. All magick, even folk candle magick, comes back on the petitioner three fold, so it is important to check into your motives before beginning any sort of spell.

# BECOME A SUPER-BEING

Casting spells uses personal energy, so be sure that your mind is not cluttered and that you are not tired, as magick often tires the practitioner. Light some incense. This enables the practitioner to attune to his psychic mind, and contact his personal energies. A good night's sleep before any candle magick will aid in using your energy to its fullest.

The next thing you will want to do is anoint your candle with oil. Remember, anointing is done by rubbing the candle in the upward motion, starting in the middle of your candle. Only rub in that direction, all the while concentrating on what you are trying to accomplish. Rub that goal into the candle. Then, starting in the middle again, rub the candle downward. Continue to rub the candle in this direction, concentrating on your goal. When you feel that the candle has been successfully oiled, the candle is now blessed.

Now is the time to light the candle. Keep your goal firmly in mind. Visualize your goal. See your goal in the fire. Continue to gaze into the fire, visualizing strongly, until you are too tired to continue. You may then leave your flame. It is important to let your candle burn all the way out. This allows the energy that you infused into the candle to be completely released. Make sure your candle can burn out safely.

Your magick won't be able to help you if your house accidentally burns down because of an unattended candle. When the spell is complete if you are trying to invoke something cast the ashes to the wind. If you are banishing, throw the remains in the garbage.

**To Reverse A Candle Spell**

Gather all melted wax, burned incense, recopy all requests used in the spell you want to reverse or stop. Gather up a gray candle. You will need reversing oil and incense. Cedar is good for both a reversing oil and incense.

On a waning Moon cast a circle of white protective light around yourself and the candle. Place the candle in the middle of an alter. A small table or desktop can be used as an alter. Place all the items from the spell you want to reverse or stop around the gray candle and say:

# BECOME A SUPER-BEING

*These things have I wrought will now cease to exist. Go back the way you have begun, cease now and desist. With harm to none and no alarm the energies dissipate. Return all things now as they were. I relinquish them to fate.*

Light the candle and allow to burn down.

### Candle Spells

Take a candle and anoint it by rubbing a drop or two of myrrh oil on it. Using a straight pin, scratch your desire into the wax and then light the candle and allow it to burn itself completely out. That's all there is to it. This is a very simple, yet highly potent spell, try it out sometime.

### Friendship Spell

To perform this spell you will need one pink candle. Some apple blossom or strawberry oil for friendship and good luck. One pink silk ribbon and one white silk ribbon.

Cast a circle of white protective light. Anoint the candle with the oil while thinking of the friends that you want to make. Imagine yourself laughing with them, going out with them. Visualize yourself with them.

Light the candle when you have finished anointing it with oil. At this point you may call out the things that are important to you in a friend: honesty, trust, open- mindedness, humor.

As you light the candle, see the flame as being the energy that burns between any two close friends. When this is completed, take your two pieces of silk ribbon and weave them together. Simply winding them around each other will do.

While you do this, think of bringing that friend closer to you. This binding process is reminiscent of pagan handfasting rituals. You are binding that friend to you, making them loyal to you, a way any good friend should be.

# BECOME A SUPER-BEING

You do not want to bind a specific person to you, as that kind of magick is harmful since it manipulates the other person's free will. Only bind the idea of the perfect friend to you. Once you have done this, tie the ribbon to the base of your candle as best as you can. The candle's light is a beacon to bring friendship to you and another person.

When this is done, you may wish to sit and meditate on the spell that you have just cast, sending your energies out to bring that perfect friend to you. When you feel that your spell has been completed, then it has. Let your candle burn all the way out and release your circle of white protective light.

### Psychic Protection Spell

In order to protect yourself from psychic attacks, you need a black, taper candle and protection oil or incense. Frankincense or Bayberry will serve as good protection incense or oil. It is best to find a work area that you can leave untouched for three days. If you must put away your tools, try to at least keep your spell candle out in the open.

Just prior to your work, bathe in purification herbs, or with your favorite bath salts. While you are bathing, concentrate again on the purpose of your spell. Do not let negative thoughts enter your mind.

After bathing, go to your work area. Cast a circle and light some incense. Envision a large, white ball of light surrounding you, your work area, and your home. Hold the candle between the palms of your hands and direct all of your positive energy into the candle. Place the candle in its candle holder. Prior to lighting the candle, say out loud or to yourself:

***This candle represents protection over me in all things. Protection in all places and in all time.***

Next, light the candle and say:

***As the light of this flame grows, I can feel the light and positive energy around me. As this candle burns, everything around me is***

# BECOME A SUPER-BEING

***blessed with light and love. I am blessed with light and love. Negative energy is being banished. Nothing can harm me.***

Sit back and watch the candle burn. Keep visualizing the white ball of light and protection around you. Envision your Higher Power blessing you and protecting you from harm. See yourself blessing whoever or whatever it is that brings harm to you. Bless them so that they may be happy and will no longer wish to cause you harm. Feel the peace and love.

When the candle has burned 1/3 of the way, say:

***As the flame of the candle is extinguished, evil, negativity, and harm towards me is banished.***

You can now end the circle of white protective light and allow the candle to burn out. Repeat this for two more nights. On the last night, after the candle has burned away and the leftover wax has cooled, discard the wax in the garbage to symbolize throwing away that which causes you harm.

You have been blessed with light, love, peace, and protection. Whatever was causing you harm will no longer do so.

### Candle Love Spell

Cast a circle of white protective light. You will need one pink candle anointed with rose oil and some patchouli incense. Light the candle and incense and cut a circle out of red or rose pink cloth. Fill it with a mixture of any of the following herbs and oils: acacia flowers, myrtle, rose petals or buds, jasmine flowers, lavender, cloves, rosemary, cinnamon, olive oil, basil, mint, patchouli, musk, honeysuckle. Add a red felt heart and a copper coin. Write in tiny letters on a small piece of paper:

***Aphrodite of the sea, Send my true love to me.***

Place the invocation along with the herbs into the circle of cloth. Charge the cloth with a protective pentagram traced in the air over its surface. Bind the charm by tying it with a blue thread in seven knots. Allow the candle to go out and open the circle.

### Healing A Broken Heart

Take three white candles and anoint them with rosemary or violet oil. Light the three candles while visualizing the one who broke your heart. Cut a small circle out of blue cloth. Place on it: feverfew, myrtle, and white rose petals.

Cut a heart out of white felt and cut it in half. You may add a copper coin if you wish to attract new love. Sew the two pieces together again with blue thread, concentrating on your desires and emotions. Place it among the herbs. Twist it into a little bag and breathe on it to charge it with air.

Pass it through the three candle flames to charge it with fire. Sprinkle it with water to so charge it. Sprinkle it with salt to charge it with earth. Hold it close to you and charge it with all of your associated visualizations. Then relax and ground the energy.

Tie the charm with white thread and bind it. You must carry the bag with you for two weeks. Keep the bag on you the entire two weeks. Even while you sleep. The bag must absorb your energies. Afterwards, burn the bag during the first new moon.

### Money, Money, Come To Me...

Using candle magick to draw money can be a very powerful spell. Great care must be taken whenever doing any kind of drawing magick, due to the possibility that your spell could accidently harm someone close to you. Always make sure you include in your ritual the command that your request will cause no harm or misfortune.

To work this candle spell you will need seven purple candles. Anoint each candle with either ginger, honeysuckle, or jasmine oil. With a new straight pin, carve on each candle your first name, and the word Money.

# BECOME A SUPER-BEING

Visualize yourself receiving money through a new job, a pay raise, winning a contest. Never visualize cash just appearing to you, generally because that money will have to come from someone else, usually a poor, unfortunate relative. Light all seven candles while saying with each candle:

***Money, money, come to me.***

Allow each candle to burn itself out. Gather up the remains and bury close by.

## Making Your Own Candles

If you are so inclined, crafting your own candles for the purpose of magickal spells can be a satisfying and spiritually rewarding hobby, as well as helping the energies along by infusing the candles with your own personal vibrations.

The following is a list of things you'll need to make your own hand dipped candles: a double boiler or a long coffee can or similar substitute, paraffin wax, wicks, crayons, essential oils and herbs appropriate to the purpose of the candle. The amounts of these depends on how many candles you plan to make. It is suggested that you try and make only a few candles at first.

Fill a pot with enough water to surround half of the can you are using and bring to a boil. Cut up the wax into slices and place in can. Reduce heat and carefully place the can in the center of the pot. As the wax is melting, stir it frequently with a wooden spoon.

When the wax is melted, add the crayons and mix until they have completely melted and the color is consistent. The color of the candle will be a bit lighter than the wax in the can or pot, so adjust it accordingly. Add the desired herbs and oil and mix again.

Cut the wick to the length you want leaving an extra two inches for the dry wick. If you want to make two candles at once double the length. You will probably need only an extra three inches as they are easier to hang. Dip the ends of the wick in the wax and allow to dry. Keep repeating the process until it has sufficient weight to fully sink into the wax.

# BECOME A SUPER-BEING

With every dip charge the candle with your intent and allow it to completely dry between each dip. To make an average size candle you will probably have to dip it at least 30 times. Hang to dry and enjoy. There you go, your own candles to which you've added your own personal energies.

Another type of candle that you can make is a beeswax candle. A sheet of beeswax looks like a honeycomb. Beeswax makes a good candle when the particular ritual or spell you are doing requires that no animal fat be burned.

To make a beeswax candle, simply roll the beeswax sheet around a candle wick. The way to do this is to place the beeswax sheet on a smooth flat surface. You'll want to cut the sheet at the size of the candle that you wish to make. Now press the wick vertically onto the shorter side of the beeswax and roll the sheet around the wick. The final result is a natural beeswax candle that would make any candle magick practitioner proud.

Candle magic is such a simple, natural way to invoke the energies of the universe that some forget to put their mind to the process. It is always important to achieve a good, reflective state of mind when performing candle magic. Anything that interferes with your ability to concentrate and achieve the high energy state necessary to perform candle magick should be avoided. Such as, screaming children, a sink full of dirty dishes, use of alcohol or drugs, etc. Plus, you should avoid scattering your energy by attempting to do more than one magickal working at a time.

Remember that Magick is the manipulation of energy, a thought is a form of energy and a visualization is an even stronger form of energy. Your visualization can be a method used to intensify further and direct your will. Your visualization can be the method by which you control the magickal energy you have produced. You must know what you want. You must see it. You must feel the high energy flow. You must direct it with your thoughts. This is why you must learn to control your thoughts so that they do not control you.

One of the most important elements in the practice of any form of Magick is the Universal Law of Cause and Effect. This means that whatever you do (or don't do) you cause something to happen. The next most important consideration is the Universal Law of Retribution. This means that no matter what you do, it comes back to you in like kind. It is the nature of things that as you send something out it gains momentum, so that by the time it comes back to you, it is

## BECOME A SUPER-BEING

three times stronger. If you do something nice for someone, someone will do something nicer for you.

As you weave and spin your spell. Three fold return the tale will tell.

# BECOME A SUPER-BEING

# BECOME A SUPER-BEING

### CHAPTER EIGHT – MAGICK CRYSTALS AND PRECIOUS STONES

*Trust that as you remain faithful to your inner search you will be told all things you have need of.*

### Annie & Byron Kirkwood

IT is believed that the use of crystals have been with us since the beginning of time. Quartz (silicon dioxide), is a naturally occurring mineral existing in about 80 per cent of the earth's crust. Ancient civilizations secretly reserved the crystal for use by the religious hierarchy, royalty, military leadership and secret societies. Popular legends and the psychic readings of Edgar Cayce all point to the use of "power crystals" called Tuaoi, or "Fire Stones" in Atlantis.

Allegedly, power crystals were large crystals that were used to generate power for the ancient civilization. The abuse of the crystal energies were believed to have caused the downfall and final destruction of Atlantis. It has also been suggested that crystals helped the Egyptians move the huge limestone blocks to build the pyramids. Crystals may have been used to light inner tunnels and chambers while the pyramids were being constructed. Ancient Egyptians carved sacred figures and ornate drinking vessels from crystals. The ancient Greeks believed that quartz came down from Olympus and was called the "eternal, or holy, ice."

The Gods supposedly poured holy water down from the heavens to benefit mankind. As the water fell through the air it became frozen, becoming valuable rock crystal. The Greeks used the natural magnifying power of quartz to light their ceremonial fires. It is said that focused crystal heat was used to cauterize

# BECOME A SUPER-BEING

wounds and heal the sick. However, no physical evidence has ever been uncovered to support these claims.

Native Americans also have a legend explaining the close connection that crystal has with mankind. This story comes from the Cherokee nation. The ancient people lived in harmony with Nature. They spoke the same language as animals and plants. They hunted only to satisfy their hunger and needs. Almost always, they offered prayers of thanks for what they had taken from nature. And nature always provided what was needed.

As time went on humans lost their innocence and harmony. They took more than what they needed and forgot to offer prayers of thanks. They began to kill animals and humans for sport or pleasure. The Bear Tribe, chief among the animals called a meeting of all animals They decided something needed to be done. The Bears suggest that they shoot back at the humans that shot at them, but the bow and arrow required that great sacrifice, for one bear had to give up his life so that his sinew could be used as bowstring. But the claws were way too long for shooting the arrows anyway.

The Deer Tribe, wanted to bring disease into the world, each one would be responsible for different illness. When the humans forgot to give thanks before eating the food they had killed they would get sick. Each animal decided to invoke a different disease.

The Plant tribe was a little more sympathetic and felt that disease was way too harsh of a punishment, so they decided to present the humans with a cure. If the people used their intelligence, they would be able to find cures for their ailments and regain their balance.

All of Nature agreed on this plan. One herb spoke out, this was Tobacco and he said he would be the sacred herb, he would not cure a specific disease but would help people return to the sacred way of life. The close friends of the Plant Tribe were the Rock & Mineral Tribes, they agreed to help also. Each mineral would have its own spiritual power, a vibration that when used would regain perfect health.

The chief of the tribe Quartz Crystal put his arm around his friend Tobacco and said "I will be the sacred mineral and will heal the mind. I will help bring wisdom and clarity in dreams, see the origin of disease and record spiritual history, so humans will be able to gaze into me and may see the origin and the way of harmony."

It is so today. Research has shown that crystals are superb amplifying reflectors, capable of vibrating when excited by energy. Because of these qualities, silicon crystals are used in computers, communications and laser technology. For example, quartz crystals are used in microcircuits to amplify electrical signals in microphones, as well as being used to transform electricity into radio and television broadcast signals.

Science has shown how effective quartz crystal can be as an energy boost. As we humans are walking energy fields, crystals are important agents in harnessing our energy to heal and enhance our spiritual, psychic and intuitive abilities. Crystals have electromagnetic power, or piezoelectric properties. This can intensify the human electromagnetic field, or aura, that we all have, helping to clarify thoughts, channel energy, and heal. The flow of electrons through the crystal, combined with its ability to resonate with, amplify, and transmute your own personal energy shows how crystal can be such a powerful and positive energy tool for working on the human mind, body and spirit.

### Selecting A Crystal

When you are ready to pick the crystals that best resonate your personal energies, first spread your choice of crystals in front of you. Then, close your eyes while moving your hand over the minerals available. As you run your hand over the crystals, the ones that resonate with your vibrational field will start a pulse in the palm of your hand. It will get faster the closer you get to the crystal. You might also feel a pleasant heat.

Once you have narrowed it down, then cup the crystals in your palm, one hand over the other and communicate with your possible stones to make sure they are right for you. Your right crystal will set your palms pulsating big time and you will know that you have chosen correctly. Crystals can work for its owner almost indefinitely. As long as you remember to occasionally charge up your crystals with your personal vibrations, then your crystals should give you many years of wonderful service. Also, while it may seem like a good idea at the time, don't lend your stones to anyone else.

# BECOME A SUPER-BEING

## Cleansing your Crystal

Once you get your crystal home, you will want to cleanse it. Many people will handle the crystals before you acquire them. You want to make sure that all vibrations from others have been cleared. When you are ready to program your desire and energize, the crystal will be yours and yours alone.

The simplest way is to place the crystal in direct full sunlight for a day, three days or even a week. Most will be clear after a day of soaking of the rays. Remember to bring them in at dusk, then you can put them back out in the sunlight the next morning.

Next you use moving water, if you have a stream near your home you place them in the moving water for a day or two. You may also use pure, filtered water. Fill a bowl with water saying "I purify you with water." Visualize the water washing the crystal clean, leave it in the water for a short time.

You can smudge your crystal with Sage. Light the sage and move your crystal through the smoke, at the same time saying that you cleanse them. You can also place the crystal on a bed of sea salt for twenty-four hours.

For crystals that have been abused, you may want to bury them for at least seven days in the earth. You can keep them buried for as long as needed. If you are close to the ocean you may take a crystal to the shore and cleanse it in sea water. Visualize sending a beam of white light from the third eye and surround your crystal, sweeping away all negativity with the tide. These are just a few of the many ways that can be used. Remember, use whatever method feels comfortable to you. There really is no right or wrong way.

## Turning On A Crystal

A crystal, like a radio receiver, must be turned on for it to work. Of course this doesn't mean you have to blow in its ear or bring it flowers. Instead, it must be activated by a source of electrical energy. As a crystal user, you can do this by wearing it next to your body, or, better yet, by grasping in your hand. Wrapping your fingers around a crystal causes it to react to energies received from living cells and your brain's mental output. It then starts vibrating on a frequency in harmony with your body and brain.

# BECOME A SUPER-BEING

Upon receiving pulsed messages from its energy source, the crystal amplifies and broadcasts them outward in spiral waves of energy information. If the crystal is efficient, these messages may be received by your body's cells, the subconscious and the conscious mind. Much may be subliminal and received mostly by the subconscious and body cells, which may or may not relay it to the conscious mind.

A knowledgeable crystal user can usually get the subconscious to cooperate and deliver the information. You are now ready to program your crystals. To begin, sit in a quiet place where you know you will be undisturbed , cup your crystal in your hand, right over left.

Start by meditating with your crystal, feel the vibrations. Become one, instruct your crystals, giving them precise directions. Ask the crystal for guidance, protection and assistance.

Repeat your directions as many as 20 30 times. Each time you a building a energy field. Direct the energy field for 30 60 seconds and allow the program to enter the crystal. Your intuition will tell you when your crystal is ready.

### Crystal Magick

There are three necessities in Crystal Magick, without these three items you will not succeed.

**1. The Need:** A need must exist. It cannot be satisfied through any other means. A need is an empty space in your life or critical condition which must be worked on immediately.

**2. The Emotion:** Emotion is power. If you are not emotionally involved in your need, you will be unable to raise sufficient power from any source and direct your need. The emotion sets the power free to bring the need into manifestation

**3. The Knowledge:** The technique which we use to obtain the energy within ourselves or stone, to send forth the magical need. The knowledge includes visualization, concentration and the reality of power.

# *BECOME A SUPER-BEING*

Once the need, emotion and knowledge are present, you can effectively begin using crystal magic. An excellent way to benefit from crystal magick is by wearing your crystal. A crystal is usually worn around the neck, stimulating the thyroid and increasing the efficiency of the immune system. A crystal also assists the respiratory system and helps sooth sore throats. When the crystal is pointing down it is grounding, soothing and calming. Giving energy to all systems. When pointing upwards this strengthens the spirit and gives a general uplift. A double terminated crystal (pointed at both ends), is great to use as it balances the two, giving a combination of both.

### Banishing Anger With Crystal Magick

This spell is best performed beside flowing water. Cast a protection circle by imagining a glowing circle of protective white light surrounding you. Take your crystal and cup it in your hands allowing your personal energies to infuse the mineral. Raise it to your forehead, concentrating all of your anger and projecting it into the stone. Take the crystal and place it in a small, unused, cloth bag. Dunk the bag, crystal and all, into the running water three times, each time saying: With this stone Anger be gone. Water bind it, No one find it.

Take the crystal out of the bag and visualize it opening a "door" through the protective circle. After which you may recite:

*The circle is open, But unbroken, May the peace of the universe, Go in my heart.*

After a spell like this, it is always advisable to thoroughly cleanse and re-charge your crystal for future use. Care must be taken that each time you "use" your crystal it should be clear of any past influences.

### Amethyst Crystal Spell When Emotionally Upset

This spell is best used when emotionally upset, dumped by a lover, ending a relationship, stressed to the point of severe mental problems or other unstable conditions. The amethyst crystal to be used for this spell will be thrown away, so make sure that you use a stone that you aren't especially attached to.

Go to a place outside where you will not be disturbed. Take a amethyst crystal and hold it in your left hand (or right hand if you are left handed). Pour out your feeling and emotions from your body down you arm, out your palm and into the stone. Feel every pain, every emotional hurt and send it directly to the stone with your total being.

When the stone is bursting with all the negativity, take and throw the stone as far as you can with as much force as you can. Raise your voice and shout as loud as you can as you throw the stone. When your hand releases the stone, release your hurt with it. Know that the pain is in the stone, that the emotions are now outside of your body and no longer a part of you.

Calm down, breathe deeply, mediate a few moments, thank the Earth for its help then turn and leave your problems behind you. The Earth will absorb the hurt, leaving the stone free, but never take the stone back. Never think of your hurt again.

### Crystals As A Way Of Life

Crystals are extremely effective as an amplifier of various types of magick and magickal spells. The process is simple. Whenever you use folk magick, keep your favorite crystals somewhere on your body. It helps if your crystal is directly touching your skin, that way the crystal can resonate with your thought vibrations. You can also make an alter out of a small circle of crystals.

Arrange your crystals around your candles, incense, herbs, or whatever type of spell you are currently conducting. Not only do the crystals serve as a focusing agent, they also provide a shield of protection around your spell to guard against any negative energies

Crystals should be a part of anyone's life if they intend to use folk magick. The benefits of keeping crystals far outweigh the minor inconveniences that arise from the proper care and maintenance of healthy crystals. Much as you would care for a pet, crystals require loving care and attention on a daily basis. This

# BECOME A SUPER-BEING

doesn't mean you have to take them for a walk, or keep their water dish filled. Instead, it means you have to keep them free of dust or other contamination.

You should handle a crystal everyday to keep the vibrational bond between you strong and unsullied. Never allow anyone else to handle your favorite crystals. Keep several "unbonded" crystals on hand for friends who simply can't resist touching the beautiful stones.

If you follow these directions, you should get years of pleasure from your crystals. Not only for their magickal abilities, but also from the exquisite beauty that all crystals contain within them. There are few things that can rival the delicate splendor of the morning sun reflecting the rainbow from the facets of your freshly charged crystals.

### Crystals And Sacred Stones In The Bible

The use of crystals and sacred stones for mystical purposes was common among the peoples of the Holy lands. Called amulets, these magical charms were made in the form of small pendants attached to a necklace or bracelet. They were worn to protect The a person from negative energies, evil and injury, and also to bring good luck.

In the Old Testament there were twelve sacred gemstones that came from the Mountain of God, where Moses received the Ten Commandments. They were given to Moses, whose blueprint for a sacred breastplate for his brother, the high priest Aaron, is given in Exodus, 28:15-21:

> *And thou shalt make the rational of judgment with embroidered work of divers colors, according to the workmanship of the ephod, of gold, violet, and purple, and scarlet twice dyed, and fine twisted linen. It shall be four square and doubled: it shall be the measure of a span both in length and in breadth. And thou shalt set in it four rows of stones. In the first row shall be a sardius stone, and a topaz, and an emerald: In the second a carbuncle, a sapphire, and a jasper: In the third a ligurius, an agate, and an amethyst: In the fourth a chrysolite, an onyx, and a beryl. They shall be set in gold by their rows. And they shall have the names of the children of*

# BECOME A SUPER-BEING

*Israel: with twelve names shall they be engraved, each stone with the name of one according to the twelve tribes.*

The Jewish Encyclopedia says that the vestments of the high priest were interpreted in three ways. The explanation of Philo is as follows ("Vita Mosis," iii. 209): His upper garment was the symbol of the ether, while the blossoms represented the earth, the pomegranates typified running water, and the bells denoted the music of the water. The ephod corresponded to heaven, and the stones on both shoulders to the two hemispheres, one above and the other below the earth. The six names on each of the stones were the six signs of the zodiac, which were denoted also by the twelve names on the breastplate. The miter was the sign of the crown which exalted the high priest above all earthly kings.

Josephus' explanation is this: The coat was the symbol of the earth, the upper garment emblemized heaven, while the bells and pomegranates represented thunder and lightning. The ephod typified the four elements, and the interwoven gold denoted the glory of God. The breastplate was in the center of the ephod, as the earth formed the center of the universe; the girdle symbolized the ocean, the stones on the shoulders the sun and moon, and the jewels in the breastplate the twelve signs of the zodiac, while the miter was a token of heaven.

Many of these same gemstones are listed in Ezekiel, Chapter 28 in reference to the King of Tyrus. Said to have the power to summon angels; the book of Ezekiel, Chapter 28:13-16, calls them "The Stones of Fire."

There is the mention of the use of two onyx stones, along with 12 stones in the breastplate, and the mention of two very mysterious stones called the Urim and Thummim which were used to divine the will of God. These two mysterious stones are kept within the breastplate, and so the breastplate is called the "breastplate of judgment."

There are also twelve gemstones listed in Revelation, Chapter 21. These sacred gemstones are: Jasper, Sapphire, Chalcedony, Emerald, Sardonyx, Sardius, Chrysolite, Beryl, Topaz, Chrysoprasus, Jacinth, and Amethyst.

Many scholars believe that the gems are the same twelve "Stones of Fire," that were in Aaron's Breast Plate of Judgment. In St. John the Divine's vision of the Heavenly Jerusalem, the City stood on a foundation of 12 stones, each correlating with one of the stones of the breast plate. The stones, though, are in a

# BECOME A SUPER-BEING

different order – with the last stone of the breastplate (the stone associated with the tribe of Benjamin) listed first.

According to some, the literal reason for these vestments was that they denoted the disposition of the terrestrial globe; as though the high-priest confessed himself to be the minister of the Creator of the world, wherefore it is written (Wis. 18:24): "In the robe" of Aaron "was the whole world" described. For the linen breeches signified the earth out of which the flax grows.

The surrounding belt signified the ocean which surrounds the earth. The violet tunic denoted the air by its color: its little bells betoken the thunder; the pomegranates, the lightning. The ephod, by its many colors, signified the starry heaven; the two onyx stones denoted the two hemispheres, or the sun and moon.

The twelve precious stones on the breast are the twelve signs of the zodiac: and they are said to have been placed on the rational because in heaven, are the types of earthly things, according to Job 38:33: "Dost thou know the order of heaven, and canst thou set down the reason thereof on the earth?" The turban or tiara signified the empyrean: the golden plate was a token of God, the governor of the universe.

In the 1913 book *The Curious Lore of Precious Stones*, author George F. Kunz recounts the early beliefs of Andreas, bishop of Caesurae, who lived in the last half of the 10th century C.E. Andreas was one of the first to associate with the Apostles of Jesus the symbolism of the 12 gemstones.

**The Jasper**, which like the emerald is of a greenish hue, signifies St. Peter.

**The Sapphire** is likened to the Heavens (from this stone is made a color popularly called lazur) and signifies St. Paul.

**The Chalcedony** may well have been considered what we now call the carbuncle and represented St. Andrew.

**The Emerald**, which is of a green color, is nourished with oil that its transparency and beauty may not change; this stone signifies St. John the Evangelist.

**The Sardonyx**, which shows a certain transparency and purity of the human nail, represents James.

# BECOME A SUPER-BEING

**The Sardius** with its tawny and translucent coloring suggests fire and represents Philip.

**The Chrysolite**, gleaming with the splendor of gold, symbolizes Bartholomew.

**The Beryl**, imitating the colors of the sea and air, and not unlike the jacinth, suggests Thomas.

**The Topaz**, which is of a ruddy color, resembling somewhat the carbuncle, denotes Matthew.

**The Chrysoprase**, more brightly tinged with a gold hue than gold itself, symbolizes St. Thaddaeus.

**The Jacinth**, which is of a celestial hue, signifies Simon.

**The Amethyst**, which shows to the onlooker a fiery aspect, signifies Matthew.

On pages 289-301 of Kunz's book, there is information concerning the ancient names of the stones and what they are named today. In the following list, the ancient or biblical name is given, followed by the modern name in parentheses. They are:

Sardius (Carnelian), Topaz (Peridot), Chalcedony (Emerald), Emerald (Almandine garnet), Sapphire (Lapis Lazuli), Sardonyx (Onyx), Jacinth (Agate), Amethystos (Amethyst), Chrysoprase (Citrine), Agate(Agate), Jasper (Jasper), and Onyx (Turquoise).

The last item to consider about the 12 stones is the significance of color. The colors or patterns are, as recounted by Andreas: green, blue, red, translucent tan, orange, golden, sky blue, purple.

The colors of the stones have their own Christian symbolic meaning:

**Green:** Canonical color for use on Sunday. Hope, joy, and the bright promises of youth.

**Blue and Sky Blue:** An emblem of the Celestial regions and Celestial virtues. In Christian art, the Virgin, Saints, and Angels are often depicted in blue robes.

# BECOME A SUPER-BEING

**Red:** This color is used in ceremonies concerned with the Pentecost, and at various religious feasts. It suggests and symbolizes suffering and martyrdom for the faith, and the supreme sacrifice of Christ upon the Cross. Divine love and majesty are also typified by this color.

**Dull yellow or tan:** The color has a connotation of treachery and envy. Hence Judas was dressed in dull yellow or tan clothing. Heretics were required to wear clothing of this hue when they were condemned to the stake in medieval times.

**Orange and golden yellow:** This color is emblematic of God's goodness and of faith and good works. The color of the sun from the beginning of man's recognition of things spiritual has had major significance.

**Violet:** A canonical color which is appropriate for use during Lent, and on Advent Sunday, along with Septuagesima and Quinquagesima Sundays. The chastening and purifying effects of suffering find expression in this color.

## The Power of Crystals and Gemstones

Even though it is not listed as one of the 12 stones, crystal was an important gemstone in the Holy land. In the Bible, crystal was referred to under a number of different names. Hebrew **ghbsh** (Job 28:18), **qrh** (Ezekiel 1:22): both words signify a glassy substance; Septuagint gabis; Vulgate eminentia (Job 28:18); **krystallos, crystallus** (Ezekiel 1:22). — This was a transparent mineral resembling glass, most probably a variety of quartz. Job places it in the same category with gold, onyx, sapphire, glass, coral, topaz, etc. The Targum renders the **qrt** of Ezech. by "ice"; the versions translate by "crystal."

Crystals and gemstones can hold and convey power, spiritual energy; they can amplify and serve as vehicles of energy, and can be vehicles of spiritual energy, Divine Power. This is especially true of gemstones and crystals, the expression of the highest of life in the mineral realm.

All gemstones and crystals have a capacity to hold and convey spiritual energy, but among any kind of gemstone or crystal are those that have a very special or extraordinary capacity to do so – it is as though they are blessed or "charmed," as though they were specifically destined for sacred use, spiritual work; these are the stones we seek and use in our art of divine theurgy or wonderworking.

Among crystals there are different forms, different shapes, different kinds – and they may be used for different theurgic operations, different divine works. A "generator" does exactly what the term implies – it generates a field of energy-intelligence or light-power extending into the space around it; it is a whole natural crystal, usually cut at its base, which stands upright freely, usually of some size and substance. In Sophian teachings these are called "great stones," "key stones," "cornerstones" or "earth-keepers," and larger ones have also been called "archangelic stones,"

When we invoke light-power, the divine powers, in a theurgic working, these stones serve as material talismans of the spiritual energy – they become a physical vehicle and matrix of the divine force invoked, as though an interface between the spiritual energy and the material dimension.

The direct influx of the divine powers can be too intense and overwhelming for many individuals; in terms of the Creative Force, there are relatively few individuals who can receive the direct influx and not become swiftly overwhelmed. Crystals, however, can be used like power transformers, serving to downgrade the influx of Divine Power, making it accessible to more individuals.

Experiencing and receiving something of the Divine Power at a lower grade, of course, can serve to upgrade a person's energy and soul, and thus facilitate the experience and reception of Divine Power at a higher grade – in other words the use of crystals is skillful means, a help along the way, as with many tools we use, even the spiritual practices themselves.

This was the very purpose of the stones used in the outfit of the high priest – an interface of the Divine Power with the material dimension and a downgrading of the Divine Power making it accessible at a lower level. According to the Holy Torah, the Divine Power flowing from the ark of covenant was so intense that even if the most righteous person touched it, with good intention, they would fall dead. So, indeed, whatever the Divine Power that was moving among them, there was a need to bring it down to a material level when communicating to the people.

# *BECOME A SUPER-BEING*

In the Kabbalah the knowledge and wisdom of the use of sacred stones and sacred places in the earth corresponds to Archangels Uriel and Sandalfon, and to the Divine Name of Adonai – it is part of the wisdom of Malkut, the Shekinah display of Malkut of Malkut.

### Preparing A Crystal For Bible Verse Magick

When it comes to using crystals or gemstones, personal preference on what type of stone to use is generally the best course to follow. Most people do not have a wide range of different types of gemstones to choose from before attempting a magick spell. By no means does this suggest that you cannot use these spells with other types and colors of gemstones. Again, personal preference is the key here. You may find that your personal energies resonate best with a moonstone, or a piece of pink tourmaline, so feel free to experiment with a wide variety of stones if you have them at your disposal.

The practitioner can try one of the 12 sacred stones of fire from the Bible, or a gemstone that is one of the sacred colors. Consult the list in chapter two for other types of crystals and gemstones and their attributes. Whatever type of gemstone you decide to use, always make sure that your stone has been "cleared" before using it.

Clearing has to do with the energy of the stone or crystal. Crystals can be charged with our thought vibrations and then act on our subtle energy fields. When used with Bible verse Magick, they help to create situations in our lives that will lead us in directions that allow positive growth and healing.

Clearing a crystal or gemstone is a simple task, and it is a way to insure that there are no left over energies from a previous spell. It is a way to reprogram your crystal, and create a new energy bond for each and every spell.

There are many ways to do this, but this is a simple and effective way; first, make sure you will not be disturbed. Next, hold your crystal under running water, and as the water pours over it, close your eyes and imagine all the negative energies are washed away down the drain and out to the vast ocean to be purified by the cycles of life. You can also leave your stone in the warm sun, and allow the power of light to purify the crystal. Another excellent method is to burn a little sage and pass your gemstone several times through the smoke. To charge your new crystal for a new Bible verse spell, you are encouraging or awaking the stone to help you or someone else with the properties it possess. By charging, you are asking for a specific kind of help and you let the stone know which powers you need.

Charging is simply done by holding the stones in your projective hand (right if right handed - left if left handed), visualizing your magical need, and pouring energy out from your body into the stone. Once you can feel the vibrations - you know that the stone has been charged. As with any Bible verse spell, before you begin make sure that you have some time to yourself where you will not be disturbed by any sort of distractions. Take the phone off the hook and lock yourself away in a quiet room with the lights turned down. If you desire, you can play a little soft music to enhance the mood.

Sit quietly for a while and concentrate on what it is that you want your spell to accomplish. Hold your crystal in your hands and try to visualize the energies of your desire combining and resonating with the energies of your stone. If it helps with visualizing your desire, write down on a clean piece of white paper what you want to achieve.

When you are ready, say the Bible verse once out loud. For added power, repeat two more times for a total of three times. Afterwards, sit quietly for a few more minutes thinking about your desire and what you want to accomplish with it.

If you feel that your spell has been successful, that is all you have to do. If, however, it feels incomplete, you can repeat the same spell with the same crystal for six more days, a total of seven. If after three week have passed and you still have not received an answer to your spell, consider that the Universe may have other plans for you and a spell would be interfering with that fate. Wait about a month and try again if you so desire. Or you may want to change the wording of your desire to clarify what exactly you want to happen.

Take your paper and pen and write down what your fears are. Write about your anger, helplessness, and the craziness of your life, or in the lives of those you wish to protect. Write down every word of how you feel about the situation(s). Feel the stone taking on those things which frighten you or on those things that

# BECOME A SUPER-BEING

you wish to have protected. When you are through, hold the crystal and let its energies overwhelm you and feel its strength making you stronger.

### CRYSTAL SPELL TO INCREASE LOVE BETWEEN A COUPLE

Suggested gemstone: **rose quartz**

*Finally, brethren, whatsoever things are true, whatsoever things are honorable, whatsoever things are just, whatsoever things are pure, whatsoever things are lovely, whatsoever things are of good report; if there be any virtue, and if there be any praise, think on these things.*

Philippians 4:8

### CRYSTAL SPELL FOR NEW ROMANCE

Suggested gemstone: **alexandrite**

*It was but a little that I passed from them, When I found him whom my soul loveth: I held him, and would not let him go, Until I had brought him into my mother's house, And into the chamber of her that conceived me.*

The Song of Solomon 3:4

### CRYSTAL SPELL TO HAVE SOMEONE NOTICE YOU

Suggested gemstone: **calcite**

*So that thou incline thine ear unto wisdom, and apply thine heart to understanding;*

Proverbs 2:2

# BECOME A SUPER-BEING

## CRYSTAL SPELL FOR RECONCILIATION

Suggested gemstone: **sapphire**

*I love them that love me; and those that seek me early shall find me.*

Proverbs 8:17

## CRYSTAL SPELL TO GET BACK A LOVER WHO IS WITH SOMEONE ELSE

Suggested gemstone: **agate**

*Therefore shall ye lay up these my words in your heart and in your soul; and ye shall bind them for a sign upon your hand, and they shall be for frontlets between your eyes.*

Deuteronomy 11:18

## CRYSTAL SPELL TO REMOVE NEGATIVE FEELINGS FROM YOUR HEART

Suggested gemstone: **topaz**
Depart not hence, I pray thee, until I come unto thee, and bring forth my present, and set it before thee. And he said, I will tarry until thou come again.

Judges 6:18

## CRYSTAL SPELL TO GET OUT OF A BAD SITUATION

Suggested gemstone: **carnelian**

# *BECOME A SUPER-BEING*

*Our soul is escaped as a bird out of the snare of the fowlers: the snare is broken, and we are escaped.*

Psalms 124:7

### CRYSTAL SPELL TO BRING HOPE AND COMFORT

Suggested gemstone: **hematite**

*For thou didst cast me into the depth, in the heart of the seas, And the flood was round about me; All thy waves and thy billows passed over me.*

Jonah 2:3

### CRYSTAL SPELL TO EASE THE HEART

Suggested gemstone: **calcite**

*And it shall come to pass, when many evils and troubles are come upon them, that this song shall testify before them as a witness; for it shall not be forgotten out of the mouths of their seed: for I know their imagination which they frame this day, before I have brought them into the land which I sware.*
Deuteronomy 31:21

### CRYSTAL SPELL TO FIND JOY

Suggested gemstone: **amethyst**

*But they that escape of them shall escape, and shall be on the mountains like doves of the valleys, all of them mourning, every one for his iniquity.*

Ezekiel 7:16

# BECOME A SUPER-BEING

### CRYSTAL SPELL TO KEEP BAD LUCK AT BAY

Suggested gemstone: **cat's-eye**

*The LORD is my shepherd; I shall not want.*

Psalms 23:1

### CRYSTAL SPELL TO REMOVE EVIL EYE

Suggested gemstone: **moonstone**

*But let him that glorieth glory in this, that he understandeth and knoweth me, that I am the Lord which exercise loving kindness, judgment, and righteousness, in the earth: for in these things I delight, saith the Lord.*

Jeremiah 9:24

### CRYSTAL SPELL TO REMOVE CURSES

Suggested gemstone: **opal**

*My tongue also shall talk of thy righteousness all the day long; For they are put to shame, for they are confounded, that seek my hurt. - Psalms 71:24*

### CRYSTAL SPELL TO TURN ENEMIES INTO FRIENDS

Suggested gemstone: **turquoise**

And ye shall chase your enemies, and they shall fall before you by the sword.

Leviticus 26:7

# BECOME A SUPER-BEING

### CRYSTAL SPELL TO PREVENT ATTACK AND THIEVES

Suggested gemstone: **chrysoprase**

*If a soul sin, and commit a trespass against the LORD, and lie unto his neighbor in that which was delivered him to keep, or in fellowship, or in a thing taken away by violence, or hath deceived his neighbor;*

Leviticus 6:2

### CRYSTAL SPELL TO STOP LIES AND DECEIT

Suggested gemstone: **sardonyx**

*The Lord judge between me and thee, and the Lord avenge me of thee: but mine hand shall not be upon thee.*

1 Samuel 24:12

### CRYSTAL SPELL TO REGAIN PEACE AFTER AN ARGUMENT

Suggested gemstone: **sunstone**

*I have trodden the winepress alone; and of the people there was none with me: for I will tread them in mine anger, and trample them in my fury; and their blood shall be sprinkled upon my garments, and I will stain all my raiment.*

Isaiah 63:3

### CRYSTAL SPELL TO STOP PERSECUTION FROM KNOWN AND SECRET ENEMIES

Suggested gemstone: **peridot**

# BECOME A SUPER-BEING

*All that found them have devoured them; and their adversaries said, We are not guilty, because they have sinned against Jehovah, the habitation of righteousness, even Jehovah, the hope of their fathers.*

Jeremiah 50:7

## CRYSTAL SPELL TO FIGHT OFF PSYCHIC ATTACK

Suggested gemstone: **obsidian**

*Oh that thou wouldest rend the heavens, that thou wouldest come down, that the mountains might quake at thy presence.*

Isaiah 64:1

## CRYSTAL SPELL FOR SAFETY

Suggested gemstone: **lepidolite**

*But we were gentle in the midst of you, as when a nurse cherisheth her own children.*

1 Thessalonians 2:7

## CRYSTAL SPELL TO REMOVE A BINDING SPELL

Suggested gemstone: **malachite**

*Because of his strength I will give heed unto thee; For God is my high tower.*

Psalms 59:9

# BECOME A SUPER-BEING

## CRYSTAL SPELL TO PROTECT ALL LOVED ONES

Suggested gemstone: **amethyst**

*But God shall wound the head of his enemies, and the hairy scalp of such an one as goeth on still in his trespasses.*

Psalms 68:21

## CRYSTAL SPELL FOR GOOD LUCK

Suggested gemstone: **apache tear**

*Sing unto Jehovah a new song, and his praise from the end of the earth; ye that go down to the sea, and all that is therein, the isles, and the inhabitants thereof.*

Isaiah 42:10

## CRYSTAL SPELL FOR SEVEN DAYS OF GOOD LUCK

Suggested gemstone: **staurolite**

*Yea, thou doest away with fear, And hinderest devotion before God.*

Job 15:4

## CRYSTAL SPELL TO CHANGE YOUR LUCK

Suggested gemstone: **green aventurine**

## *BECOME A SUPER-BEING*

*And on my behalf, that utterance may be given unto me in opening my mouth, to make known with boldness the mystery of the gospel.*

Ephesians 6:19

### CRYSTAL SPELL TO FIND SOMETHING THAT WAS LOST

Suggested gemstone: **agate**

*For he bringeth down them that dwell on high; the lofty city, he layeth it low; he layeth it low, even to the ground; he bringeth it even to the dust.*
Isaiah 26:5

### CRYSTAL SPELL TO OVERCOME SHYNESS

Suggested gemstone: **tourmaline**

*Behold now, I have opened my mouth; My tongue hath spoken in my mouth.*

Job 33:2

### CRYSTAL SPELL FOR CLARITY OF THOUGHT

Suggested gemstone: **chrysocolla**

*And now, behold, the hand of the Lord is upon thee, and thou shalt be blind, not seeing the sun for a season. And immediately there fell on him a mist and a darkness; and he went about seeking some to lead him by the hand.*

Acts 13:11

# *BECOME A SUPER-BEING*

## CRYSTAL SPELL TO SEE THE FUTURE IN DREAMS

Suggested gemstone: **amazonite**

*In a dream, in a vision of the night, When deep sleep falleth upon men, In slumberings upon the bed;*

Job 33:15

## CRYSTAL SPELL TO GAIN GREAT HONOR

Suggested gemstone: **labradorite**

*If a man therefore purge himself from these, he shall be a vessel unto honour, sanctified, and meet for the master's use, and prepared unto every good work.*

2 Timothy 2:21

## CRYSTAL SPELL TO GET RID OF EVIL SPIRITS

Suggested gemstone: **bloodstone**

*And Jesus rebuked him, saying, Hold thy peace, and come out of him. And when the devil had thrown him in the midst, he came out of him, and hurt him not.*

Luke 4:35

## CRYSTAL SPELL TO RESIST TEMPTATION

Suggested gemstone: **pietersite**

# *BECOME A SUPER-BEING*

*Enter not into the path of the wicked, and go not in the way of evil men.*

Proverbs 4:14

## CRYSTAL SPELL FOR PERSONAL PROTECTION

Suggested gemstone: **staurolite**

*For thou hast been a refuge for me, A strong tower from the enemy.*

Psalms 61:3

## CRYSTAL SPELL FOR SUCCESS IN THE LOTTERY

Suggested gemstone: **sapphire**

*And take double money in your hand; and the money that was brought again in the mouth of your sacks, carry it again in your hand; peradventure it was an oversight:*

Genesis 43:12

## CRYSTAL SPELL FOR WEALTH AND PROSPERITY

Suggested gemstone: **citrine**

*Bring ye all the tithes into the storehouse, that there may be meat in mine house, and prove me now herewith, saith the Lord of hosts, if I will not open you the windows of heaven, and pour you out a blessing, that there shall not be room enough to receive it.*

Malachi 3:10

# BECOME A SUPER-BEING

## CRYSTAL SPELL TO BANISH DEBT

Suggested gemstone: **iolite** (also known as **cordierite**)

*He that receiveth a prophet in the name of a prophet shall receive a prophet's reward: and he that receiveth a righteous man in the name of a righteous man shall receive a righteous man's reward.*

Matthew 10:41

## CRYSTAL SPELL FOR SUCCESS WITHOUT HURTING OTHERS

Suggested gemstone: **malachite**

*He that hath knowledge spareth his words: and a man of understanding is of an excellent spirit.*

Proverbs 17:27

## CRYSTAL SPELL TO BE MORE RESPONSIBLE WITH MONEY

Suggested gemstone: **aventurine**

*The Lord of hosts hath sworn, saying, Surely as I have thought, so shall it come to pass; and as I have purposed, so shall it stand:*

Isaiah 14:24

## CRYSTAL SPELL TO LOOK BEYOND MATERIAL POSSESSIONS

Suggested gemstone: **ametrine**

# BECOME A SUPER-BEING

*Lay not up for yourselves treasures upon the earth, where moth and rust consume, and where thieves break through and steal:*

Matthew 6:19

## CRYSTAL SPELL FOR GREATER SPIRITUAL UNDERSTANDING

Suggested gemstone: **amethyst**

*And it shall come to pass in the last days, saith God, I will pour out of my Spirit upon all flesh: and your sons and your daughters shall prophesy, and your young men shall see visions, and your old men shall dream dreams:*

Acts 2:17

## CRYSTAL SPELL TO OPEN YOUR THIRD EYE

Suggested gemstone: **sodalite**

*Even the mystery which hath been hid from ages and from generations, but now is made manifest to his saints:*

Colossians 1:26

## CRYSTAL SPELL TO SEE THE TRUTH

Suggested gemstone: **azurite**

*And art confident that thou thyself art a guide of the blind, a light of them which are in darkness,*

Romans 2:19

# *BECOME A SUPER-BEING*

### CRYSTAL SPELL TO KNOW YOUR GUARDIAN ANGEL

Suggested gemstone: **celestite** (also known as **celestine**)

And the *angel that talked with me came again, and waked me, as a man that is wakened out of his sleep,*

Zechariah 4:1

### CRYSTAL SPELL TO INCREASE PSYCHIC POWERS

Suggested gemstone: **sugilite**

*And the Lord shall guide thee continually, and satisfy thy soul in drought, and make fat thy bones: and thou shalt be like a watered garden, and like a spring of water, whose waters fail not.*

Isaiah 58:11

### CRYSTAL SPELL TO RECEIVE DIVINE GRACE, LOVE AND MERCY

Suggested gemstone: **seraphinite**

*Let the heavens be glad, and let the earth rejoice: and let men say among the nations, The Lord reigneth.*

1 Chronicles 16:31

### CRYSTAL SPELL FOR GREATER WISDOM FROM GOD

Suggested gemstone: **sapphire**

# BECOME A SUPER-BEING

*For nothing is hid, that shall not be made manifest; nor anything secret, that shall not be known and come to light.*

Luke 8:17

## CRYSTAL SPELL TO SEND GODS BLESSINGS TO SOMEONE ELSE

Suggested gemstone: **citrine**

*But they that wait upon the Lord shall renew their strength; they shall mount up with wings as eagles; they shall run, and not be weary; and they shall walk, and not faint.*

Isaiah 40:31

## CRYSTAL SPELL TO HELP A FRIEND FIND PEACE

Suggested gemstone: **jade**

*The Lord hear thee in the day of trouble; the name of the God of Jacob defend thee;*

Psalms 20:1

## CRYSTAL SPELL TO END A BAD SITUATION

Suggested gemstone: **aventurine**

*Heap on wood, kindle the fire, consume the flesh, and spice it well, and let the bones be burned.*

Ezekiel 24:10

# BECOME A SUPER-BEING

### CRYSTAL SPELL TO SEE THE TRUTH

Suggested gemstone: **agate**

*Therefore speak I to them in parables; because seeing they see not, and hearing they hear not, neither do they understand.*

Matthew 13:13

### CRYSTAL SPELL TO BE TRULY HAPPY

Suggested gemstone: **peridot**

*A man' belly shall be satisfied with the fruit of his mouth; and with the increase of his lips shall he be filled.*

Proverbs 18:20

### CRYSTAL SPELL TO KEEP AWAY THOSE WHO WOULD HURT YOU

Suggested gemstone: **chrysoberyl** (cat's eye)

*For he shall be like the heath in the desert, and shall not see when good cometh; but shall inhabit the parched places in the wilderness, in a salt land and not inhabited.*

Jeremiah 17:6

### CRYSTAL SPELL TO HELP A FRIEND IN A BAD SITUATION

Suggested gemstone: **amber**

# *BECOME A SUPER-BEING*

*Wherefore let them that suffer according to the will of God commit the keeping of their souls to him in well doing, as unto a faithful Creator.*

1 Peter 4:19

### CRYSTAL SPELL TO END A SICKNESS

Suggested gemstone: **quartz crystal**

*And the people, when they knew it, followed him: and he received them, and spake unto them of the kingdom of God, and healed them that had need of healing.*

Luke 9:11

### CRYSTAL SPELL TO HEAL A FRIEND

Suggested gemstone: **rhodonite**

*What is it then? I will pray with the spirit, and I will pray with the understanding also: I will sing with the spirit, and I will sing with the understanding also.*

1 Corinthians 14:15

### CRYSTAL SPELL TO HEAL YOUR AURA

Suggested gemstone: **labradorite**

*It is the spirit that quickeneth: the flesh profiteth nothing. The words that I have spoken to you, are spirit and life.*

John 6:63

# BECOME A SUPER-BEING

## CRYSTAL SPELL TO HEAL ALL WOUNDS

Suggested gemstone: **red/banded agate**

*Therefore, thus says the Lord GOD, 'Because you have made your iniquity to be remembered, in that your transgressions are uncovered, so that in all your deeds your sins appear--because you have come to remembrance, you will be seized with the hand.*

Ezekiel 21:24

### Guide For Crystals and Gemstones

**Agates:** Strengthens mind and body.

**Banded Agate:** Protective; re-energizes the body, lends courage, Relieves spastic discomfort.

**Black Agate:** Protective; wear for success in competition and for courage.

**Black and White Agate**: Wear as an amulet to protect against physical danger.

**Blue Lace Agate:** Balances the psychic centers. Helps relieve despair, depression, helps with other strong emotions.

**Brown Agate:** Success, can also be worn as a wealth talisman.

# BECOME A SUPER-BEING

**Green Agate:** Good for healthy eyes. Can also be used to induce psychic powers, especially the ability to see great distances. Red Agate Heals the blood; promotes peacefulness and calmness.

**Amber:** Helps purify the body. Good for healing, love, beauty, strength, good luck. Amethyst Enhances psychic ability, calms, relieves stress. Healing, good for dream work and meditation, peace. Relieves headaches, enhances mental ability.

**Bloodstone:** Physical healing, detoxifies the blood, good for headaches, high blood pressure, and self confidence.

**Blue Topaz:** Clears and focuses the mind, excellent for inspiration.

**Citrine:** Detoxifies the body, psychic awareness. Boosts healing energy, creativity, energizing.

**Diamond:** Increases personal clarity. Good for healing of body and soul.

**Emerald:** Good for eye diseases, dreams, and meditation. Love, peace, understanding.

**Flourite:** Good for nervousness, receptiveness to other stones. Raises IQ to highest possible capacity.

**Garnet:** Draws out and removes negative energy, good for strength, blood, kundalini, self confidence. Enhances the power of other stones.

**Hematite:** Draws sickness and fever from the body, stimulates the flow of oxygen through the body.

**Jade:** Good for money, wisdom, longevity, prosperity. Attracts love, helps prevent sickness, disease and tired, sore muscles.

# BECOME A SUPER-BEING

**Moonstone:** Relieves cramps, opens psychic ability, good for female problems and the birthing process. Said to draw bad energy away from whoever holds one.

**Onyx:** Relieves stress.

**Opal:** Used to see all the possibilities in a situation. Discover a broader view. Some people find this stone very hard to wear. A little opal can go a long way.

**Pearl:** Enables one to accept love. Helps see the good parts of oneself so you can love yourself and others more.

**Pyrite:** Strengthens will power.

**Quartz:** *Rose Quartz* Love, friendship, compassion. *Smokey Quartz,* Balancing. Good for meditation and dreams. *Rutilated Quartz,* (with ribbons of gold or silver in it) Cleanses arteries and veins, stimulates brain, clairvoyance.

**Sapphire:** Helps with spiritual comprehension.

**Selenite:** Soothes, inspires, nurtures the body and soul.

**Sodalite:** Calms, clears the mind, excellent for grounding rituals.

**Sugalite:** Good for healing, spirituality, promotes psychic ability.

**Tiger Eye:** Enhances self confidence, strength, and will power. Good luck, money, wealth and material happiness.

**Tiger Iron:** [mixture of tiger eye, hematite, and red jasper] Nerve strengthener, good for legs, liver, colon.

# BECOME A SUPER-BEING

**Turquoise**: Good for creativity, emotional balance, blood, nervous and respiratory systems. Excellent for healing, love, friends, money, protection, courage. Good luck to those who hold turquoise close to their heart.

## Buying Gemstones And Crystals

There are many ways that dealers treat gemstones. The savvy buyer asks lots of questions and hopefully tests the results. You should look for the quality of the stone, does it have a good color, good clarity and desired shape? Are there chips, dents, and imperfections in the stone?

You should watch out for stones that have been irradiated. This is when a stone has been exposed to radiation to enhance its color. Gemstones are dead once they are irradiated, thus making them useless for any kind of magick.

Irradiation is often used on Aquamarine, Topaz, Emerald, and Diamonds. Some dealers don't even know if they are selling irradiated stones. If you can feel energy from gemstones, it will be either very scattered or dead when a gemstone has been irradiated.

Watch out as well for fake or synthetic gemstones. If you aren't sure what a stone is, don't be afraid to ask. An honest dealer will let you know if the stone is natural or man-made. Going to Gem and Jewelry Shows exposes you to all kinds of gemstones. Find a dealer you can trust to assure you are getting the best gemstones.

# BECOME A SUPER-BEING

# BECOME A SUPER-BEING

### CHAPTER NINE – HERBS: NATURES GIFT

*Accept the responsibility for eating correctly, breathing deeply, drinking water in adequate quantities, exercising the body and keeping loving thoughts within the mind.*

**Kathy Oddenino, Joy of Health**

**Disclaimer:** This information is provided for entertainment purposes only. Your use of any of the herbs listed is strictly at your own risk and is not intended to replace the care of a licensed physician. The author and publisher of this book accept no responsibility or liability for damages resulting from your use or misuse of the information or herbal cures listed in this chapter.

**PLANTS** and people have been intertwined since the beginnings of life on Earth. Mother nature has provided both men and animals a rich cornucopia of plants and herbs that provide not only food, but healing and magickal properties as well.

Knowledge of herbs and their secrets were passed down from generation to generation by a complex oral tradition known by only a selected few. The people who knew which plants could kill, cure, distort reality, and serve as a magickal focus, were regarded with respect and some fear by the uninformed population.

Holy men and women, as well as doctors were privy to the hidden powers of natures botanical gifts. Many who were once persecuted as witches were probably skilled herbalists who had used their knowledge to help their neighbors, but were instead harassed and accused of being in league with the devil. The

# BECOME A SUPER-BEING

development of modern medical practices borrowed heavily from ancient herbal remedies. However, doctors refuse to admit the connection.

**Herb Magick**

Herbs are a powerful part of the grid of energy and matter that connects us all. Herbal magick is a ritual process in which we direct natural forces to bring about desired changes. This is a natural process, an organic art involving cooperation between the earth and the practitioner.

Ritual has been an integral aspect of human spirituality throughout the ages. Focusing your intentions and desires, with the aid of elements and organisms of the earth is a powerful, and ancient method of magic ritual. When it comes to rituals it's best to keep it simple. Elaborate rituals are fine and have their place, but often it is the simple things that pack the most magickal punch. The less steps and words to remember, the clearer your focus will be on your intent.

Before you start any herbal magick, you will first need a mortar and pestle for grinding herbs, an incense burner, charcoal disks for burning herbs, wood or ceramic mixing bowls, bottles for tinctures and oils, pieces of cloth or muslin bags and ribbon or natural fiber for making sachets and amulets, candles, a personal journal and some much needed personal space.

For your incense you might want to try making your own rather than buying it from a store. Ground herbs and raw resins are the simplest form of incense and can be mixed and tailored to any need or intention. Try to use herbs and resins in their most raw form. This way they are closest to nature and the natural forces that you want to tap into with herb magick. In addition, prepared sticks and cones can be heavily perfumed and filled with impurities.

To start, separately grind up the herbs that you would like to use in your incense. Use a clockwise motion and visualize your intent. Mix the ground herbs together in a mixing bowl with your fingers, and, while visualizing your intent hold your hands over the herbs. This process of visualization while interacting with and processing the herbs is called enchanting. Light a charcoal disk and sprinkle some of the powdered herbs onto it.

To store your enchanted herbs you will need a sachet or medicine bag. These are cloth bags or pieces of cloth filled with herbs and tied with ribbon or cord. They can be worn, placed in a home, under a pillow, given to a friend, any number of uses.

Choose a color of cloth and ribbon to suit your intention. You can also include other objects in the sachets such as crystals, stones etc. Write or draw your wish or intention on a piece of paper. Next, place the enchanted herbs that you would like to use onto the paper. Fold it up and burn it while you visualize your wish. The is also done with certain herb leaves in place of the paper. You can write your intention on a bay or sage leaf and burn it as a herbal petition.

In a powdered form, enchanted herbs are very convenient for spreading the power of herbs wherever they are needed. Often powders will consist of a mixture of salt and ground herbs. Herb magick can also be practiced using essential or infused herbal oils, massage oils, and tinctures.

## Herbal Potions

Herb Magick can be as easy as making herb tea. Your own kitchen and backyard are all that you need. Some herbs are stronger tasting than others, and some batches of the same herb are more powerful than others, so you will have to experiment.

For a basic brew, gather, grind and mix the herbs. Empower them with your goal. Put one tablespoon of dried herb (cut and sifted), or four tablespoons of fresh herb into a teapot. Add one quart boiling water. Let steep for 20 minutes.

This is long enough to extract the medicinal properties of the herbs and long enough to let the tea cool off enough to drink. Strain tea through cheesecloth and use as directed.

Milissa Deitz has compiled some of her favorite herbal potions that can be made from common herbs easily grown in any backyard garden.

## A Healing Brew

One part rosemary, one part sage, one part thyme, one part cinnamon. Half fill a blue glass bottle with fresh water. Add the ground, empowered herbs and let

# BECOME A SUPER-BEING

it sit in the sun all day. If by sunset the water has been colored by the herbs it is ready for use. If not, store in the refrigerator overnight then put in the sun the next day. Strain the mixture and anoint the body, or add to the bath water while visualizing yourself as being in perfect health.

### Potion for Passion

One pinch of rosemary, two pinches of thyme, two teaspoons of black tea, one pinch of coriander, three fresh mint leaves, three fresh rose petals, five lemon tree leaves, three pinches of nutmeg, three pieces of orange peel. Place all the ingredients in a teapot. Boil three cups of water and add to the pot.

Sweeten with honey if you desire. This potion is not guaranteed to make another person fall in love with you forever but it may relax inhibitions and mellow the emotions.

### Aphrodisiac Bath

Three parts rose petals, two parts rosemary, two parts thyme, one part myrtle, one part jasmine flowers, one part acacia flowers. Add to bath water along with three drops of musk. Bathe in this before meeting a friend or lover.

### Energy Bath

Three parts carnation, two parts lavender, two parts rosemary, two parts basil. Use when tired or depressed. Visualize the water sparkling with fiery drops of energy that melt into your body, lending you vitality and power.

### Herbal Sachets

Sachets are small bags or pieces of cloth that contain magical herbs. To make a sachet take a small amount of material, either square, rounded or triangular shaped. Place about a teaspoon of herbs in the center and sew the ends together with yarn. You can make the sachets large or small, it depends on whether it's for the home or to be carried as a personal charm.

# BECOME A SUPER-BEING

If it is a personal charm, carry it with you at all times. If it is for the house or car, squeeze it and place it in the spot where it seems to have the most energy or vibration. Some sachets ward off certain energies or disease, others will draw a specific power to you.

For most sachets, a handful or less of the empowered herb is enough to do the job. Sachets for the house are usually bigger than those that need to be carried on you. Mix the herbs and empower them with your magickal needs.

Select the appropriate cloth and cut it into the desired shape. Place the herbs in the middle, gather up the corners and tie the charm together. Replace it every 3 months or so. The ingredients from the old charm should be removed from the sachet and buried. You can also make a poppet or voodoo doll out of cloth and herbs. The poppet is made to represent the person being aided through magick. Poppets are made to speed healing, draw money, love and many other needs, though never to cause injury.

### Home Protection Sachet

Three parts rosemary, three parts basil, two parts fennel seed, one part bay, one part fern, one pinch of salt. Tie up the ingredients in a red cloth and place in the highest accessible spot in your home.

### Car Protection Sachet

Two parts juniper, two parts rosemary, one part mugwort, one part comfrey, one part caraway, one small quartz crystal. Tie up in a red cloth and put the charm in your car in a place where it won't be easily found. After a few months, take the charm apart and create a new charm. You can cleanse the crystal and re use it.

### Personal Protection Sachet

Three parts basil, two parts rosemary, two parts cinnamon, one part nutmeg, one part thyme. One small crystal charged with your personal energy. Tie up the ingredients into a small bag and tie with a natural string made from cotton or hemp. The sachet can be carried in your pocket or purse, or worn around the neck. The sachet should be small enough to be carried around easily. After three months, take the sachet apart and bury the old ingredients except for the crystal which can be cleansed and used again.

### Love Sachet

Three parts catnip, two parts dill seed, one part mint, one part rosemary. To attract love, visualize love energy coming to you as you mix the herbs. Keep the sachet close at all times and love should find you by the end of three months.

### Some Favorite Magickal Herbs

**Divination:** Cloves, nutmeg, thyme.

**Dream magick:** Cinnamon, mistletoe.

**Good health:** Allspice, coriander, ginseng, thyme.

**Good luck:** Chamomile, nutmeg, sandalwood.

**Love magick:** Basil, catnip, cinnamon, dill seed, ginger, mint, rosemary, sage, thyme.

# BECOME A SUPER-BEING

**Money:** Basil, chamomile, cinnamon, garlic, thyme.

**Protection:** Cloves, marjoram, basil, sandalwood, African ginger.

**Psychic development:** Cinnamon, rosemary, thyme.

**Success:** Basil, sandalwood.

### Alfalfa, It's Not Just For Horses Anymore

Keep in the alfalfa in your home to protect against poverty and hunger. Alfalfa is also very healthy when eaten. The taste, however, leaves much to be desired.

### A Little Basil For The Heart

While your mate is asleep, sprinkle a little basil powder over them, especially over the heart, and fidelity will bless your relationship. Keeping basil in little sachets hidden all through the house will provide domestic tranquility.

### Caraway To Prevent Carry-Away

An object holding Caraway seeds is theft proof. Seeds are also used to encourage fidelity and are placed in sachets to attract a lover. Chewing the seeds is helpful to gain the love of the one you desire. They can also strengthen the memory.

### Cloves Are Nothing To Gossip About

When burned as incense, cloves can stop gossip about you. Worn or carried, cloves attract love and romance.

# BECOME A SUPER-BEING

### Hawthorn Your Troubles Away

Hawthorn, when carried, promotes happiness in those who are troubled, depressed or sad. Brings a little magickal cheer to one's life.

### You Just Have To Respect Marigold

Picked at noon, marigold strengthens the heart. In the bath, this plant helps you gain the respect of all you meet. Good when used just before job interviews.

### Skullcap Only Has Eyes For You

When skullcap is worn in a sachet by a woman, it will help to protect her mate from the wiles and charms of other women.

### A Bit Of Spearmint Before That Big Test

When the sweet scent of spearmint is inhaled, it increases mental awareness and power. It is also good for energy during strenuous activity. Spearmint can also help your memory and aid in long term retention.

### Herbs For Love

Adam and Eve Roots need to be carried in a small bag at all times to attract love. Given to a couple, these two roots will ensure continued happiness.

Dutchman's Breeches is a root that is worn to attract love.

Elm was once known as Elven among elves, when carried it will bring a new love when none had been expected.

Other herbs for love are: maple, clover, jasmine, endive and dill.

# BECOME A SUPER-BEING

## Herbs For Money and Wealth

The leaves or Orange Bergamot are slipped into wallets and purses to attract money.

Rubbing your money with orange bergamot before spending it will ensure its return.

When Irish Moss is carried or placed beneath the outside door mat, it will ensure a steady flow of money to the household. It can be carried and used for luck by stuffing it into a sachet.

## Herbs For Wishes

To have a wish come true, carve your wish into a piece of bamboo and bury it in a secluded area. Carry a small piece of bamboo with you at all times for good luck. Bamboo can also be kept in your car to steer you clear of bad drivers.

The branches of the Buckthorn when placed near doors or windows, drives away any evil spirits and bad vibrations. To make a wish, stand in an open area, start by standing facing east, concentrate on your wish, turn towards your left and at the same time continually sprinkling the buckthorn until you have completed a full turn. This is best done at sunrise to help cleanse your personal energies.

## Herbs For Friendship

Loveseed was used by the Pawnee Indians for magickal ceremonies. Carry these seeds to attract new friendships.

Contrary to its name, the Passion flower is placed in a house to calm problems. When carrying some with you at all times, you will attract new friends and be very popular.

# BECOME A SUPER-BEING

### Herbs For Good Luck

The Aloe plant is considered to be a protective plant. It guards against negative and evil influences. If you keep the aloe plant in your house, luck will soon follow.

Grains of Paradise are used in love, luck and wishing. For love and luck, place the grains in a sachet and keep it close to you. When making a wish, take some of the herb and toss it in each direction starting in the east and ending in the west.

### Herbs For Employment

Carry a piece of Devil's Shoestring in your pocket while seeking employment. Do the same if you are having problems at work or if you are asking for a raise at work.

The root of the Orchid plant, called Lucky Hand, has been widely used in New Orleans magical botanicals. It is placed in sachets and conjure bags for good luck and general success and carried to obtain and maintain employment.

To insure you do not lose your job, obtain a small amount of pecans. Shell them. While you slowly eat them, visualize yourself working and enjoying your job. Picture yourself receiving hefty pay checks with excellent benefits every week. Take a small amount of the shells and place them where you work. Special care must be taken to choose the proper place to hide your shells. Make sure they can't be found or removed. After three months, bring in fresh pecan shells to keep up the energy.

### Herbs For Healing

The Amaranth was used by the Aztecs during rituals and in burial ceremonies. When you are feeling ill, a crown of amaranth should be worn to promote healing.

Place a barley straw around a rock and visualize your pain leaving your body and entering the straw and rock. Toss it into a river or lake and with it will go the pain. When burned as a incense, cinnamon aids in healing physically and spiritually. Cinnamon stimulates psychic powers and can be used in sachets as well.

Eucalyptus is used to promote health by using it in a sachet, poppet, or placing the leaves in and around the house. Other household herbs that a good for healing are: garlic, thyme, spearmint, onion, mint and rosemary.

### Herbs For Divination

It is said that after blowing on a dandelion, the number of seeds left are the number of years you have left to live. To tell the time, blow three times at the head of the dandelion and the number of seeds left will be the time. Take the yellow, flowering head of a dandelion and ask a YES or NO question. Drop the head into a cup of water, if the head floats, with the flower facing upwards, your answer is absolutely YES. If the flower sinks or is facing downwards, the answer is NO.

Ground Ivy can be used to discover who is working negative magic against you. On a Tuesday, place the herb around the base of a yellow candle and the person will become known to you. Write a question on a fig leaf, if the leaf dries slowly then the answer is YES, if it should dry quickly then the answer to your question is NO. As you eat an orange think of a YES or NO question you want answered. Count the seeds in the orange and if there are an even amount of seeds the answer is NO, if there are an odd number of seeds then your answer is YES.

### Herbs For Protection

Althea is used in protection rites and calming an angry person. For complete protection, burn Althea as an incense and speak out loud of what or whom you need protection from. Carve a piece of Ash wood into a solar cross (equal armed), and carry it on you at all times. A staff of ash wood placed over a door will ensure protection of your home. Cacti of all kinds offer protection, grown indoors facing the direction of your door, a cactus will guard against any unwanted intruder. For full protection place one in all directions in your house.

# BECOME A SUPER-BEING

## Herbs For Happiness

Sprinkle Witch Grass around the premises to disburse petty spirits and depression. Happiness will come to you when adding Saffron to water and cleansing your hands in it, or add saffron in sachets and keep it in your room.

## Herbs For Beauty

Immerse some Maidenhair in water, then remove. If it is kept on the person or in the bedroom it will grant you grace, beauty and love. Yerba Santa when carried on you will improve or attain beauty. This herb can also help you formulate a better attitude about yourself. True beauty lies within. Unless your mental image of yourself improves, your outer image will remain the same. Place Bracken under your pillow before going to sleep every night and you will wake up in the morning feeling refreshed and looking your best. Bracken can also be mixed with frankincense and burned as an incense before retiring. Doing so will keep you looking and feeling younger. Bracken wrapped in a sachet and buried under your bedroom window will keep your sleep free from disturbing dreams.

## Using Medicinal Herbs

The old saying "An apple a day, keeps the doctor away," is probably more accurate than most people realize. Apples are high in vitamins A and C, potassium, magnesium and two other healing substances: pectin and malic acid. Vitamins A and C are vital for wound healing and fighting infection. Potassium is important for a healthy nervous system and a regular heart rhythm. Magnesium is vital for proper digestive enzyme function and, more importantly, calcium uptake. Pectin slows the absorption of food which helps diabetics maintain more stable blood sugars. It also removes unwanted metals and other toxins.

When raw apple cider vinegar is combined with a tablespoon of honey in water and taken before meals it gears up the digestive juices and helps us get the most from our foods. The use of medicinal herbs was once widely practiced in the days when doctors were few and far between. Often, so-called "qualified" physicians used methods that were dangerous, and sometimes deadly, to their unsuspecting patients. Because of this, herbal practitioners were highly sought after for their knowledge of relatively safe healing plants and herbs.

As prescription drugs became more widely available, the use of healing herbs began to wane. Fortunately, the knowledge of what certain herbs could do health wise was written down for the use of future generations.

The appeal of healing herbs is now enjoying a resurgence in popularity. Family doctors as well are becoming better educated on the uses and effects of botanical medicines. Over the years there have been many good publications on folk remedies. Most of them are simple and inexpensive and with ingredients that are easy to find and use. Many times one has to look no further than the spice cupboard or the local farmer's market.

You should be aware that just because an herb is natural this doesn't make it automatically safe. Medicinal herbs should be considered drugs and must be handled like any other kind of medicine. Never take any kind of herb or drug until you talk it over with your health practitioner first. Many people assume that herbs are perfectly safe. This is not true, medicinal herbs can have side-effects. However, herbs can bring safe, effective relief if used properly and with care.

### Healing Herbs

To help take away the pain and swelling of arthritis you need: Two part Stinging Nettle. One part Yarrow (Achillea millefolium) leaves. One part Plantine Leaves. One part Mugwort. One part Agromony (leaves and roots).

Place the ingredients in large pot then fill with cold water. Cover the pot and boil the leaves until they appear transparent. The water should be a dark green liquid. Separate leaves from the liquid. Mix in about one cup more water. Boil the liquid down until only one quart of liquid remains, keep the pot covered. Pour hot liquid into a hot jar and seal.

You can save the leaves by placing the leaves into a sealable container and freeze until needed as a poultice. Mix one part of the liquid mix with two parts of your favorite body lotion. When you are ready to use, warm up the mixture until warm to the touch, shake well then rub into affected areas.

# BECOME A SUPER-BEING

### Help For Depression

To a base tea add one teaspoon of St. John's Wort and allow to steep for three to five minutes. The most effective base tea to use is chamomile tea. The FDA recently completed research into the effectiveness of St. John's Wort (Hypericum Calycinum) in fighting depression. The FDA has stated that St. John's Wort is an effective treatment for depression. It is available in pill form from your health food store.

A word of caution when taking St. John's wort. This herb can make you sensitive to sunlight so be sure to stay out of the direct sun whenever taking this herb.

### To Help Heal Bruises

Soak one oz. Witch Hazel leaves and twigs combined in two cups of alcohol. Strain. Use full strength on bruises. You can dilute with water and use as a mouthwash as well. A poultice of Yerba Santa is also good for severe bruises. Mash the leaves of a Yerba Santa, then soak them in water, and apply while still hot to the bruise. Cover the leaves with a clean cloth and remove when cool.

### Treatments For Burns and Sunburns

Simmer one handful of balm of Gilead buds and one handful of Marigold flowers in an enamel or glass pot with water to cover. Do not boil.

After 15 minutes remove from heat, strain and pour liquid into a clean and sterile jar. Add a layer of olive oil to keep air out of mixture. Apply freely to burned area as needed.

Simmer one handful of crushed Marshmallow root and one handful of Comfrey root in one cup of white wine in an enamel pot. Cover and simmer for 20 minutes. Strain. When cool apply to burns and sunburns.

# BECOME A SUPER-BEING

## Herbs To Get Rid Of Warts, Pimples and Corns

Get an apple and cut into as many pieces as you have warts. Rub one piece on one wart. Repeat with all warts, pimples and corns. Wrap up the apple bits in a piece of cloth, then bury the whole thing. When the apple bits have rotted, the warts will be gone.

Gather a small bucket of Dandelions, this includes stems, heads and leaves. Squeeze them to extract milky fluid which then can be applied to warts, pimples and corns.

Apply Oil of Thuja to a wart. An infusion used as a wash on the warts will work as well. (Note: Thuja is also called White Cedar).

Take a fresh Marigold, squeeze out the juice and apply it directly to a wart. Let the juice dry. Make applications until the warts fall off. You can also take some fresh Milkweed juice and apply to warts. Native Americans say that milkweed will cure warts entirely with just a few applications.

## Remedies For Smoking And Coughs

If you use tobacco products, try this instead. Chew a combination of Gentian root and Camomile flowers every time you feel the need to smoke, then try the following tea recipes. Manzanita Cider: Crush a handful of manzanita berries and bruise a handful of the leaves, and pour over two cups of boiling water. When settled, strain off the liquid and use throughout the day as a drink.

Horehound Tea: Take one oz. of the green herb, one oz. of honey, and one pint of boiling water. Cover, and set aside until cold. Drink four oz. when you are coughing.

## Wonderful Garlic

Garlic is truly a wonder herb. Eating this herb will help clear sinuses. That's why you feel better after eating spicy foods when you have a cold. The cayenne pepper helps as well. You can eat garlic raw or cooked. You can slice it into pill sized wedges and swallow them with juice or tea as if they were pills.

# BECOME A SUPER-BEING

Garlic is also excellent for clearing up itchy vaginal infections. Depending on how sore you are, you can peel a clove and use it directly as a suppository, or you can wrap it in cheese cloth to prevent direct contact with sore tissues. If the infection has just gotten started and not done much tissue damage yet, you can put the garlic into a blender with plain yogurt and blend until smooth. Then apply the garlic/yogurt mix directly on the affected area.

A garlic suppository placed against the uterus will help fight uterine infections. The garlic suppository works especially well in combination with golden seal capsules taken by mouth.

### Cayenne Pepper: Oh How It Burns So Good

Cayenne is well known for its ability to stop bleeding, though you should always seek professional medical advice for any serious injury. Apply it directly to the wound.

Try it in your socks in the winter and it will help keep your feet warm. Cayenne pepper has gained a certain amount of respectability recently. This is due to the discovery that the ingredient that makes cayenne hot is an excellent treatment for pain caused by arthritis and shingles. Use sparingly though. A little cayenne pepper goes a long way.

### Common Herbs And Their Medicinal Abilities

**Black Willow:** Common aches and pains, fevers, arthritis, kidney or bladder troubles, antiseptic, gargle and tonsillitis.

**Buckthorn:** Constipation/laxative, good as a digestive stimulant, also for gas, the liver and gall bladder/stones.

# BECOME A SUPER-BEING

**Catnip:** Stomach aches or cramps, calmative, fevers, headaches, bronchitis, digestion and an effective treatment for diarrhea. Chamomile: Mild stomach aches, digestion, gas, calmative for insomnia in children, eye wash and open sores and kidneys. Echinacea: Antibiotic (simulates the immune system), used to treat abscesses in teeth or body, lymph swellings as well as a digestive aid.

**Goldenseal:** Antibiotic, for all internal/external health problems, eye wash, female infections, sores, skin conditions, colds, viruses & infections.

**Hops:** Sleep aid, liver/digestive aid, gas/cramps; externally antibiotic for boils, tumors, swellings and skin inflammation.

**Marigold:** Use externally for sores, burns, bleeding hemorrhoids and wounds. Can be combined with oil for earaches and some minor vaginal infections.

**White Oak Bark:** Internal bleeding, vaginal infections, supreme antiseptic for wounds/skin conditions, insect bites, hemorrhoids, swollen glands, tumors, poison oak/ivy, lymphatic swelling, varicose veins, mouthwash/gum problems.

**Yarrow:** Internal bleeding, gas, diarrhea, fevers that accompany the measles, colds and flu. Effective external antiseptic.

# BECOME A SUPER-BEING

# BECOME A SUPER-BEING

**CHAPTER TEN – THE MAGICK PENDULUM**

*The intuitive mind is a sacred gift and the rational mind is a faithful servant. We have created a society that honors the servant and has forgotten the gift.*

**Albert Einstein**

**PENDULUMS** are one of the oldest and most popular forms of dowsing and divination. They are simple to learn and easy to work. A pendulum is nothing more than a balanced weight (crystal, wood, metal, plastic) on the end of a string or a chain. The dowser draws on the information in the collective unconscious and focuses that information to the pendulum in order to obtain responses to questions.

With practice pendulums can be a wonderful tool to assist in gaining insight and information about yourself, a situation or another person. Just as radios pick up information from unseen radio waves, the pendulum is a powerful antenna that receives information from the vibrations and energy waves emitted by people, places, thoughts and things.

Dowsing is best known for locating water, gold, oil, and other minerals, but dowsers have also used pendulum dowsing to find missing keys, eyeglasses, jewelry, and literally anything they put their minds to locate. Probably the best known use of dowsing is the ancient art of locating water with a forked stick or pendulum. Some U.S. marines were taught to use a pendulum in Vietnam to locate underground mines and tunnels.

In France, hundreds of physicians have used the pendulum to assist them in making diagnoses, and it is a science known as radiesthesia. For centuries, dowsing has also been called "divining" because it involves knowing beyond the five senses and predicting the future.

The pendulum can also answer any yes or no question, and people often call it "The Truth Teller" because of its accuracy. Some people say that the pendulum creates a bridge between the logical and intuitive parts of the mind and that the pendulum responds to electromagnetic energy that radiates from everything on Earth.

No one knows for certain how the pendulum works, but the important thing is that it does work. As Thomas Edison is said to have replied when asked about electricity: "I don't know what it is, but it's there, so let's use it."

A little research can find numerous references to the successes of pendulum dowsing. One good example is pendulum diviner Verne Cameron. Cameron was invited by the government of South Africa in the 1960's to use his pendulum to help them locate their country's precious natural resources, but was denied a passport by the U.S. government and forbidden to leave the United States. A few years earlier, he had demonstrated his special dowsing talent to the U.S. Navy, successfully locating on a map every submarine in the Navy's fleet. He shocked Navy officials by not only locating every American submarine, but also every Russian submarine in the world. Afterward, the CIA determined Cameron was a security risk and denied him access to travel abroad.

Today dowsers use the pendulum to locate water, gold, oil and other minerals, lost objects, missing persons or pets; schools of fish, underground pipes and leaks, faulty equipment and sources of malfunctions, health problems and solutions. The pendulum can also be used to test for allergies, the quality and freshness of food and water, chemicals, pesticides or bacteria in food, compatibility between people and places or things, charged batteries, and honesty or deceit.

Pendulums can help you find out about houses, apartments, roommates, employees, used cars, etc. There are many dowsing applications and techniques. A pendulum is a powerful tool that provides you with answers so you can make more informed choices.

**Pendulum Use Through The Ages**

# BECOME A SUPER-BEING

Dowsing and the use of the pendulum is reported to date back approximately 7000 years, however, origins are still unknown. It is accepted, however, that the Egyptians detailed images of forked rods in some of their artwork as did the Ancient Chinese kings. In Europe, it is believed that dowsing was used in the Middle Ages to find coal and other mineral deposits.

In the Bergbau Museum at Bochum Germany, there is an eighteenth century Meissen figurine of a dowser in the uniform of a miner, holding a forked stick. It can be assumed that dowsing skills came with the colonists to the new world and were the means of locating the dug wells over which, for safety's sake as well as convenience, many of the early houses were built.

The late Secretary for the American Society of Dowsers, Raymond Willey, once wrote, "The dowser was a respected member of the community and it was commonly said that a man undertaking to dig a well without consulting a dowser was a fool. It is estimated that our colonial forefathers developed several hundred thousand wells by depending on the advice of dowsers."

In the early part of this century L'Abbe Bouly, a priest from the French village of Haderlot, coined the word radiesthesia to describe the use of the pendulum. The name is a combination of the Latin radius for Aradiance@ and the Greek aisthesis for "sensitivity."

In 1922, Dr. Albert Abrams published a book about the application of the powers of the pendulum, which detailed the use of the pendulum in detecting and treating disease. In 1943, Dr. Eric Perkins, Abrams' research assistant, delivered a lecture before the British Society of Dowsers describing Abrams' initial discoveries in physiological radiations which opened his eyes to the possibilities of the pendulum's medical uses.

According to Dr. Perkins, Dr. Abrams began to realize that the human body is actually a kind of broadcasting station sending out messages in the form of high-frequency radiations from every cell, tissue, and organ. He learned that the pendulum could pick up, or tune into, these radiations and determine whether or not the vibrations indicated health or disease. Unfortunately, Dr. Abrams was scorned by most of his colleagues. Nevertheless, the doctor continued his research until his death.

**How To Use The Magick Pendulum**

# BECOME A SUPER-BEING

A pendulum is probably one of the easiest tools to learn and you can start using it almost immediately. It's extremely versatile, useful and portable. The first thing that is needed is to get a pendulum. This can be any evenly weighted object on a string or chain. Some people use a small crystal, others use a ring or even a lead fishing weight. Anything can be used just as long as it is heavy enough to hang down on its string.

When you first attempt to use a pendulum, the most difficult thing to learn is to clear your mind enough so that you focus on only the question at hand. It is important to use a pendulum in a quiet place where you can concentrate. Questions posed to a pendulum must be clear, concise and direct. It is very simple to determine your yes and no swings.

Hold the pendulum in your hand, rest your elbow on a stable surface and relax. Simply ask "Show me my yes" or state "This is my yes," you will see that the pendulum begins to swing. The direction does not matter it can be toward and away from you, side to side, clockwise etc. Watch the response.

Then ask "Show me my no" or state "This is my no" and watch the pendulum direction. It will be different from the yes. You now have a basis to work from.

Asking yes or no questions of the pendulum is a great way to practice and grow comfortable with it. Questions can be for example: "Is this the correct time to do this?" or "Is this the correct decision for me?" Try to be as specific as possible.

You can use the pendulum to answer any question having two clear choices. For example, when trying to determine the sex of an unborn baby, ask the pendulum to show the swing for a girl, and then for a boy. Then ask "Is this child a boy or a girl."

Pendulums can even be helpful in narrowing choices down. Using your regular yes and no swings ask questions like "Is this likely to occur within the next 4 weeks?" if the answer is yes, then continue "Is this likely to occur within the next 3 weeks?" and so on until your yes changes to a no. Some people get an almost instant result, others have to concentrate and practice more, but most people will get something happening in a week or so. At this point you can start asking more detailed questions.

# BECOME A SUPER-BEING

As well as seeking answers to your "Yes" or "No" questions, you can also ask for protection and help from your spirit guides and highest self. Concentrate on the question and ask for the truth. Do not concentrate on the answer you want to hear because your mind will influence the pendulum. If you don't want to know something, don't ask the question.

Practice this first and get used to using the pendulum. Test it by asking questions you already know the answer to (without thinking the answer) and then start asking other questions. Remember the pendulum is a form of channeling and may be subject to low level interference depending on your state of mind, the depth of the questions and even your location.

Another method using possibly the same abilities as the pendulum is the "rubbing method." This method has been observed being used by shamans and other holy men all over the world. All you have to do is place your index and middle fingers on a smooth, but not slick surface. While gently rubbing the surface in a circular motion say to yourself: "This means YES." When you say YES your fingers should either start to stick to the surface or remain slick. Whatever the result, this will indicate a yes answer. A NO answer will be the opposite result.

For instance, say you are trying to find your lost car keys. Rub your fingers on a table or counter while asking a series of questions. "Are my keys in a coat pocket? Are they on the floor?" etc. If your NO indication is non-stickiness, your fingers should circle with no hindrance. When you hit on the YES indication, your fingers will start to stick to the surface. This method takes a little practice, but it can be successfully used to determine any number of difficult questions.

## A Scientific Explanation?

Pendulums, divining rods, and other common dowsing devices, are the simplest forms of electroscopes. The divining rods are charged with static electricity from the dowser's own body. This static electricity can be seen quite adequately with a simple millivolt meter. The amount of voltage will vary depending on the person. A good dowser will have a high reading, "above 100 millivolts" while a poor dowser may read as low as, "0 millivolts." For men the right hand is usually a negative polarity, and the left hand is positive in polarity. These polarities are usually reversed in women.

# BECOME A SUPER-BEING

A metallic pendulum attached by a wire will take on the charge of the hand it is being held by. A pendulum held by a nonconductive string will take on the charge of the last hand which held the pendulum. The pendulum when rotating above an object of a similar charge will continue to rotate and eventually swing back and forth perpendicular to the object. This pendulum when rotating above an object of the opposite charge will start to swing back and forth parallel to the object being dowsed.

Use caution when dowsing an object you have touched. The object will usually take on the charge of the last hand that touched it. This can be demonstrated by dowsing over an object such as a table knife. Depending on which hand touched the knife last an opposite reaction of the dowsing device will be seen.

To discover the depth of a water stream underground some dowsers use a long rod made of plastic, metal, or a fresh cut poplar pole. This pole is held by one end near the located underground stream, the other end of the rod is allowed to oscillate up and down directly over the stream. The number of oscillations are counted and this is the approximate number of feet below the earth where the water will be found.

This action can also be demonstrated, by realizing that the rod is just a pendulum working in a vertical plane rather than a horizontal one. To duplicate this action, place a charged object on a table. Swing a pendulum back and forth a few feet away in the same horizontal plane, counting the number of oscillations. By moving the pendulum closer or farther from the object the number of oscillations will decrease or increase.

The theory is that a static electric wave or pulse is being sent to the object being dowsed. This charge is being reflected back from the object being dowsed, and when it reaches the pendulum again as the same charge it stops the oscillations, because like charges repel. Once you have become familiar and comfortable, you can work with the many pendulum charts available, or even make them yourself. Charts can cover topics ranging from physical direction, to relationships, to holistic healing alternatives. Now, many people are finding it a subtle means of deciding between YES and NO with many questions that before would have gone unanswered. With time and practice a pendulum can become one of your most valuable magical tools. The only limits you have on the pendulum's use, are the limits of your imagination.

# BECOME A SUPER-BEING

**CHAPTER ELEVEN – MAGICK FROM AROUND THE WORLD**

*Follow your bliss.*

**Joseph Campbell**

**IN** the days before patriarchal religions had spread across the lands, the world was a mysterious place. There were wonders everywhere as gods, spirits, demons and other mysterious beings and weird energies permeated the land, seas and sky. The few people who managed to stay alive were clustered together in small groups that were kept widely separated by hundreds of miles of inhospitable wild-lands.

Life was hard and the ability to survive was precariously balanced, always ready at the slightest misfortunes to tip over into complete desolation. Even though life was difficult, the living Earth had provided a young humankind with everything that was necessary to live and even prosper. The same wild forests that could bring death in an instant, also produced an abundance of fruits, nuts, berries, succulent roots and small animals.

The vast grasslands teemed with large game animals that not only provided meat, but whose pelts were used to make clothing, blankets, even covers for huts. Humans in those days were keenly aware of everything around them. They realized that they were part of a much larger chain of existence that depended on every link to survive.

Early man was not only aware of the physical world around them, they were also cognizant to the fact that there was an invisible world that existed right alongside the material world. A world that was also linked to man's chain of existence. From these early awakenings to the unseen worlds around them, human beings quickly developed the first forms of spirituality and magick.

# BECOME A SUPER-BEING

As humans spread across the globe, they brought with them their rich and varied traditions of magick and spells. Over the centuries these isolated forms of folk magick have developed and evolved into a loosely knit confederation of practitioners. These people hold in esteem the continuation of folk magick's tradition and culture.

Possibly because it provides a link with ancestors long gone, and an affirmation of cultural worth. Folk magic has been practiced for tens of thousands of years, and it is still used today. Some say its continuance is due to its practitioners' desperate need to believe that it is effective. Folk magickians say that it's still with us because it works.

## The ABRACADABRA

One of the most famous of all talismans, and used as a magickal formula by the Gnostics in Rome; ABRACADABRA was used for invoking the aid of beneficent spirits against disease, misfortune and death. Sammonicus, the celebrated Gnostic physician, instructed that the letters of this magical triangle which he used for curing fevers, were to be written on paper, folded into the shape of a cross, worn for nine days suspended from the neck, and, before sunrise, cast behind the patient into a stream running eastward. It was also used as a charm in the Middle Ages. During the Great Plague, 1665, great numbers of these amulets were worn as supposed safeguards against infection.

A B R A C A D A B R A
B R A C A D A B R
R A C A D A B
A C A D A
C A D
A

This spell is still in use today for curing illness and gaining love or wealth.

## BECOME A SUPER-BEING

**Spell For Locating Lost Items**
*Bound and binding,*
*Binding bound,*
*See the sight, hear the sound.*
*What was lost is now found,*
*Bound & binding,*
*Binding bound*

**Bulgarian Folk Spell**


**An Invisibility Charm**
*A magic cloud I put on thee*
*from dog*
*from cat*
*from cow*
*from horse*
*from man*
*from maiden*
*till I again return.*


**Scotland Swedish Charm Against Fevers**

If someone has sharp pains, take the fruit of the beech when it starts to grow and place it in pure water while saying: "*By the holy womb of the holy Incarnation, thanks to which God has made man, you, sharp pains, and you, fevers, lessen and weaken your cold and your heat in this man.*" Then, give him this water to drink. Do this for five days and if he has a daily fever or ague, he will be quickly cured.

# BECOME A SUPER-BEING

**Casting Out Evil Spirits**
*Leave, cursed slug From man,*
*Because you have already dirtied him,*
*Now that you live in him,*
*You are the cause of great pain.*
*The sun hates you, the moon hates you*
*The stars hate you, the stars hate you,*
*Man hates you, children hate you,*
*The whole family hates you,*
*and me, I hate you.*

**Scottish Incantation**

**Reversing A Spell**

Take a mirror and simply turn completely around with the mirror reflecting outward and chant:

*Circle of reflection,*
*Circle of protection,*
*May the sender of all harm,*
*Feel the power of this charm.*

**Spanish Charm**

# BECOME A SUPER-BEING

**German Charm Of Protection Against Bad Spells**
*Eye will see you, Tongue will speak of you;*
*Heart will think of you -The Three are protecting you -*
*The Father, Son and Holy Ghost.*
*(name of sufferer inserted here)*
*His will be done.*
*Amen.*


**Russian Shape-Shifting Spell**

This spell/incantation is from Russia, pre 1900's, and was found in an 1865 book called: The Book of Werewolves by Sabine Baring Gould. The Russians call the werewolf ('thropes' in general) 'oborot' which translated as 'one transformed.' Because of this, the spell should work for all forms of animal shape-shifting. Spells and incantations allowing a magickian to alter their human body into the form of an animal have been found dating as far back as prehistoric times.

The text is as follows: "He who desires to become an oborot, let him seek in the forest a hewn down tree; let him stab it with a small copper knife, and walk round the tree, repeating the following incantation":

*On the sea, on the ocean, on the island, on Bujan,*
*On the empty pasture gleams the moon, on an ashstock lying*
*In a green wood, in a gloomy vale.*
*Towards the stock wandereth a (shaggy wolf),*
*Horned cattle seeking for his (sharp white fangs);*
*But the (wolf) enters not the forest,*
*But the (wolf) dives not into the shadowy vale,*
*Moon, moon, gold horned moon,*
*Check the flight of bullets, blunt the hunters' knives,*
*Break the shepherds' cudels,*
*Cast wild fear upon all cattle,*
*On men, all creeping things,*

# BECOME A SUPER-BEING

*That they may not catch the (grey wolf),*
*That they may not rend his warm skin!*
*My word is binding, more binding than sleep,*
*More binding than the promise of a hero!*

Then he springs thrice over the tree and runs or flies into the forest, transformed into a wolf.

### Lithuanian Charms Charm For Banishing Sickness

*Early, I wake, With bitter dew,*
*I wash, To the sun, I address myself,*
*I glorify God.*
*Sicknesses facing me,*
*Go in the dry trees,*
*The deep swamps,*
*There where no man walks,*
*There where no animal wades,*
*There where no bird flies.*

### Charm To Protect Against Venomous Snakes

*It is by fate that our difference is born, rue,*
*Fate has made us meet, rue,*
*Be not evil, Rue,*
*Do not suffer, Rue,*
*Show proof of your kindness, Rue.*
*Show proof of your kindness from now,*

## BECOME A SUPER-BEING

*From this day,*
*From this sigh.*
*Show proof of your kindness, Rue,*
*We thank you, Rue,*
*With our beautiful words, Rue,*
*With our beautiful words, Rue.*


**Charm To Stop Bleeding**
*Valiuli Dievuli, stops the blood,*
*Do not hunt the spirit of the body,*
*So that it does not leave with the blood,*
*That it does not leave the body alone.*
*By the hard stone,*
*by the high oak,*
*Valiuli Dievuli, by the blood,*
*I order,*
*I contain the blood in the veins.*


**Charm For Banishing Fever**
*In the name of the sun,*
*In the name of Perkunas,*
*By thunder, I command you, fever,*
*I hunt you from men,*
*from animals,*
*from birds,*

# BECOME A SUPER-BEING

*from each living being,*
*To the green forest,*
*the deep pools,*
*the somber swamps,*
*There where the sun does shine,*
*Where no man walks,*
*Where no animal wades,*
*Where no bird flies.*
*If you do not obey me,*
*I will dry you on the rays of the sun,*
*I will wear you out with the intensity of the sun,*
*I will drown you in the bitter dew,*
*I will feed you bewitched bread.*
*I order you to leave (name the patient)*
*To no longer torment him (or her).*

### Jamaican Magick Protection Bottle

Get a glass jar such as a Mason jar, or even a baby food jar, anything that has a lid that can be sealed tightly will work. Fill the jar halfway with small sharp objects such as pins, metal scrapings, broken glass, razor blades, etc.

Once the jar is half full with these objects, fill the jar up with a holy water mixture of salt and water. Put the top on the jar and be sure it's secured. This jar should be buried in the ground at least twelve inches deep.

As long as the bottle remains in the ground, you will be protected from harm that is sent your way. If you bury the jar some place where you won't know if it will still be there in a year, then be sure to repeat this process each year to keep the protection coming.

# BECOME A SUPER-BEING

**Old English Chant to Remove A Spell**
*Spell, spell, spell be gone.*
*Back to which ye belong.*
*Back to the caster,*
*take your disaster.*
*Spell, spell, spell be gone.*


**Mexican Charm Of Protection Against Bad Spells**
*Eye will see you,*
*Tongue will speak of you; Heart will think of you*
*The Three are protecting you*
*The Father, Son and Holy Ghost.*
*(name of sufferer inserted here)*
*His will be done.*
*Amen.*


## The Charms Of Hildegard von Bingen

**Against Mental Illness:** If someone falls ill with paralysis and one of those sicknesses that increases or decreases according to the moon, as with the case for lunatics, you must find a place where a donkey has been killed or where one has died on its own, or where it is still rolling on the ground: make the patient lie down on the ground for a short time, covered by a blanket; he or she will sleep, if they can; then take his or her hand and say: *Lazareth slept and rested, then he raised; and, just as he was pulled by Christ from his disgusting stench, you also relieve yourself of this harmful sickness and these changing fevers, you who finds yourself in the situation where Christ was found, sitting on this kind of*

# BECOME A SUPER-BEING

*donkey at the entry to Jerusalem, before the resurrection of Lazareth, meaning he would redeem man of his sins and would straighten him.*

A few minutes later, start over in the same place, and do this three times; then three times the following day or two days later; then three times again the following day or two days later, and he or she will be healed.

### Against Possessions

If a man is possessed by a crafty spirit, another man must make a sapphire fall on the earth, then put a bit of this earth in a leather pouch, he must hang it around the patient's neck while saying: *O you, unspeakable spirit, leave this man immediately, just as, during your first fall, the bright light of your splendor has gone as quickly as possible far away from you.*

This crafty spirit will be violently tortured and distanced from this man (at least if it does not concern a very aggressive or very wicked spirit) and the patient will improve.

### Against uncontrolled loves

And if even the devil pushes a man to desire a woman, to such point that, without magical practices and invocations to demons, he becomes mad with love, and if that is disagreeable for this woman, let her pour a bit of wine on a sapphire three times, each time saying: *I spill this wine on your fiery forces so that, just as God took away your shine when the angel sinned, take away the fiery love that this man feels for me.*

If the woman does not want to do this, another man who feels threatened by this love can do it in her place, he will make him drink the wine on an empty stomach or not, whether he tells him or not, and this must last for three days in a row. And if it is a woman who has a burning passion for a man, and that, for him, this love is disagreeable, he must act on the woman with wine and a sapphire as I have described it above, and the fire of the passion will burn out.

# BECOME A SUPER-BEING

## Remedies And Incantations Against Bewitchments

If someone has been bewitched by the devil, or by magic, take the same wood that is at the center of this tree (the cypress), hollow it out with an auger and then collect, in an earthen jug, water from a living source by making it flow through the hole in the wood. While pouring say: *I pour you, water, through this hole and in this virtuous virtue, so that, thanks to the force that is in your nature you flow in this man whose senses are bewitched, and so that you destroy all contradictions that are in him, and that you straighten him, and give him back the just feelings and just knowledge that God gave him in the first place.*

Let this water be given to drink on an empty stomach, for nine days because he is tormented by the devil by ghosts or by magic, and he will get better. During the nine days, this formula must be recited in the same manner.

## Another Charm Against Bewitchments

If someone is bewitched by spells or by magical formulae, to the point that he or she loses reason, you must take hot rye bread and split the crust at the highest part in the form of a cross, without dividing the loaf completely; then slip the precious stone (the hyacinth) along the length of the crack and say: *Let God, who removed from the devil, when he went against his commandment, the bright light that he pulled from precious stones, pull from you, (name) all the spells and magic formulae, and let him free you from the pain of this madness.*

Then, while sliding this same stone from one side of the bread to the other, add: *Just as the devil, because of his sin, saw his bright light removed from him, in the same way, let the madness that torments (name) because of spells and magical formulae, be removed by you and disappear.*

To finish, make the patient eat the part of the bread that is the length of the crack where the hyacinth has been placed.

# BECOME A SUPER-BEING

### Charm Against Fevers

If someone has sharp pains, take the fruit of the beech when it starts to grow and put it in pure water while saying: *By the holy womb of the holy Incarnation, thanks to which God has made man, you, sharp pains, and you, fevers, lessen and weaken your cold and your heat in this man.*

Then give him this water to drink. Do this for five days and if he has a daily fever or ague, he will be quickly relieved. After five days, if the patient is not quickly relieved, gather fresh beech fruit and repeat the charm a second time. Make sure you repeat the charm exactly the way you did it before. If he does not recover, God does not want to free him.

### Charm To Heal Jaundice

When the leaves of the beech have not yet returned completely, go near this tree, seize a branch with your left hand, and holding a small knife with your right hand, say: I cut your tartness, because you purify all the biles that lead man on paths of wrong doing and injustice; by the living word that made man without regret.

With your left hand, hold a branch while you say this, then cut it with a steel blade and keep this branch the entire year; and do this each year. If during the year, someone suffers from jaundice, cut some bits of this branch, put them in a small vase, sprinkled with a bit of wine three times, each time saying these words: *By the holy womb of the holy Incarnation, thanks to which God has made man, take from this man the pain of jaundice.*

Then heat the wine with the small branches that you have cut, in a pan or a pot and give this drink to the patient on an empty stomach, for three days, and he will be healed, unless God does not want it.

### Charm Against Migraines

If you suffer, in your head, from several sicknesses and weaknesses, to the point of becoming mad, you must put a sardonyx on the nape of your neck, in your bonnet, with a linen or leather pouch; and you must say: *As God rejected the first angel in the abyss, let him also take away from you, (name) this madness, and let him return to you your good sense.*

Repeat this every hour and you will be healed.

### Charm To Ease Delivery

If a pregnant woman, overwhelmed by pains, is not able to deliver, you must rub her thighs with a sardonyx and say: *Just as you, stone of sardonyx, have shone on the first angel by the order of God, in the same way, you, child, come shine as a man who lives in God.*

Then, she will place this same sardonyx at the baby's exit, to the exit of her sex, and she will say: *Open, paths and doors, just as for the appearance by which Christ, God, and man, has appeared and has opened the doors of hell; and you, baby, cross this door without dying and without making your mother die.*

At this moment, you must place this stone in a belt around her, and she will be eased and the baby born safely.

### Charm Against Obsessions

If a person is disturbed by demonic thoughts, night and day, awake or asleep, he must use a belt made of elk hide, and another of deer skin, and connect them with four small steel points, so that one of the belts is on the stomach, one on the back, and one on each of the sides. When he joins them at the point on the stomach, he must say: *By the power of the all powerful God, I swear to you my protection.*

When he puts the point on the back in place, he must say: *By the power of the all powerful God, I bless you to my protection.*

When he puts the point that will be on its straight side in place, he must say: *By the power of the all powerful God, I order and ordain you to my protection.*

# *BECOME A SUPER-BEING*

Finally when he puts the point that will be on his left side in place, he must say: *By the power of the all powerful God, I attach to you my protection.*

### Charm Against Madness

If someone goes mad, or is in some way prey to fantasies, you must rub a magnet with your saliva, and, with the stone, rub the nape of his neck, then his forehead, then the crown of his head. You must do this while he is quiet and peaceful. Then you should say: *Bad madness, yield to this power by which God has transformed the devil's power into kindness for man, sent forth from the high sky.*

### Charm To give Life To A Dying Patient

Find a beech root that is breaking through the ground, remove the outer bark of this root and cut it in such a way that you can do it in one cut and say: *By the first revelation in which God sees a man in the Mambré root, break the waves of poison in this man and push death away from him.*

Cut as much as you can with a second cut and say the same words; in the same way, make a third cut in this same root, so that it does not fail you during the year, and you will keep it throughout the year and you will do this each year. And when, during the year, someone has some boilings in their body, take a small piece of these cut roots and put it in a vase. You will then pour a bit of water over it three times, each time saying these words: *By the first manifestation during the was pure.*

Give the *course of which God was baptized in the Jordan, push death away from this man, thanks to this remedy, and remove all of his apparent stains, just as the life of Jesus* water to the patient to drink on an empty stomach for three days, and prepare it each time as was said: *he will be thus liberated from these boilings, unless God does not prevent it.*

The charms of Hildegard von Bingen were originally chronicled by Yves Kodratoff.

## BECOME A SUPER-BEING

Write us for our free catalog of fascinating books and other items of a very unusual nature:

Global Communications
P.O. Box 753
New Brunswick, NJ 08903

mrufo@hotmail.com

www.conspiracyjournal.com

# BECOME A SUPER-BEING

## HERE ARE THE LATEST MYSTICAL SECRETS FROM FAMED HUNGARIAN BORN PSYCHIC MARIA D'ANDREA, REVEALED IN HER NEW BOOK AND VIDEO DRAMATIZATION

### TURN AN ORDINARY GLASS OF DRINKING WATER AND AN INEXPENSIVE CRYSTAL INTO A POWERFUL ELIXIR FOR IMPROVED GOOD HEALTH, ENHANCED PSYCHIC ABILITIES AND THE FORTIFICATION OF INNER STRENGTH

Just about everyone has their favorite crystal or gemstone these days. Anyone who believes in the power of nature's most beautiful "gifts from God" realizes that there is power in them there stones. It has been scientifically proven that they can be used as psychic energizers and to greatly enhance one's life and bring about amazing benefits. **The Old Testament**, for example, is rich in references to crystals and gemstones. The breastplate of Aaron was made up of 12 gemstones, including emerald, beryl, topaz, sapphire, agate, onyx, jasper, amethyst, lapis and turquoise. These stones seemingly embraced all of the colors of the spectrum and were used to absorb or repel the radiation emitted from the Ark of the Covenant which had stored up the energy of an atomic bomb.

But do you know how to get the most out of your favorite crystal or gemstone? You can't just hold it in your hand and say abracadabra – you need to know the proper way to energize and enhance the powers that are stored up inside. Maria D'Andrea, Hungarian born psychic and shaman through the pages of her latest book and a video dramatization will teach you how to unlock the enormous vibrations that you have at your very own fingertips with a simple "trick" that includes just using an ordinary glass of tap water.

Maria's SECRET MAGICKAL ELIXIRS OF LIFE workbook and DVD study guide kit contains everything you need to know to "pump up the power" of what may seem to be ordinary stones that can be found right outside your door, turning them into highly personal talismans. The importance of a stone's shape is also described as well as what the color of a particular stone signifies. You will even find out the necessity of wearing certain crystals and gems during specific times of the week due to their astrological connections, as ruled by the magnetism of the planets.

### MAGICAL STONES

Just about every type of stone has relevance in God's order of things. "Special Blessings" and protections can come to the wearer of a crystal or stone, if worn while repeating certain prayers or performing simple rituals.

Such stones can be utilized when business is bad...when you need to take a purification bath...when you need to receive information about another person...when money is needed...when you wish to attract good luck...find a new friend., or a potential lover.

You will be given specific rituals using stones that the author says can bring you great prosperity...can help in meditation...can promote harmony around you...can strengthen the user spiritually, and can grant all your wishes. There are instructions on how to turn an ordinary glass of tap water into the "Fountain of Youth" with one of the formulas given in this book. And best of all, these "Magickal Stones" need NOT be expensive gems like diamonds or rubies. In most cases, they are ordinary stones which have little – or no – monetary value and which you can easily obtain on your own.

### PREDICTING THE FUTURE

Fortune tellers and diviners have always been with us. In addition to various forms of crystals, other stones can also be used to peer into the future. Using Maria's proven methods, the reader will learn how to have prophetic dreams with stones, how to pick up psychic vibrations from other people using crystals and gemstones, and how to see into the future in order to guide and shape your own life, as well as the lives of perfect strangers and those closest to you.

### BIRTHSTONES AND WEDDING RINGS

Find out which stones are best suited for you according to your individual birthday and what engagement or wedding ring you should give or receive to enhance the relationship. Maria D'Andrea's **SECRET MAGICKAL ELIXIRS OF LIFE** is guaranteed to add great meaning to your life and is of importance to every person who would like to increase their position in the cosmic arrangement of things.

ORDER NOW!

Your copy of **SECRET MAGICKAL ELIXIRS** book and DVD kit awaits you. To order just send $25.00 + $5.00 shipping and handling to:

**TIMOTHY G. BECKLEY, BOX 753
NEW BRUNSWICK, NJ 08903**

---

### AMAZING BENEFITS OF GEMSTONES

MARIA'S SECRET MAGICKAL ELIXIRS OF LIFE WILL TELL YOU HOW TO BE ABLE TO EASILY ASCERTAIN WHICH STONES ARE BEST SUITED FOR...

O Healing Purposes;
O Telepathy;
O Strengthening The Aura;
O Attracting A Lover;
O Obtaining Money And Prosperity;
O Controlling The Weather;
O Magnifying Your Desires;
O Shedding All Worries And Anxieties;
O Protection From Negativity;
O Bringing Courage To The Holder;
O Winning A Court Case;
O Use As An Elixir.

---

**ALSO AVAILABLE — SPECIALLY PREPARED GEMSTONE KIT YOU CAN USE WITH MARIA'S BOOK & DVD**

. This kit contains green agate, amethyst, carnelian, citrine, hematite, green jasper, rose quartz, green quartz, clear quartz, sodalite, and tiger's eye, as well as a vial of lavender oil and a blue bag to carry the kit in when you travel.

MARIA'S BOOK, DVD AND GEMSTONE KIT —
All items this page just $45.00 + $7.00 S/H

## BECOME A SUPER-BEING

# OTHER VALUABLE BOOKS BY MARIA D'ANDREA
## – ALL LARGE FORMAT WORKBOOKS · EACH INCLUDES A BONUS DVD –

**( ) HEAVEN SENT MONEY SPELLS
– DIVINELY INSPIRED FOR YOUR WEALTH**

Find out why Maria is called "The Money Psychic." Imagine receiving money just by using the powers of your mind. Want a new home? Or pay off an existing mortgage?

Would you like to go on an exotic "dream" vacation with someone who is sexy or your true love? Want to sell the items laying around in your garage or attic for BIG CASH? Interested in picking a large prize lottery ticket, or winning at the tables or slot machines?

Tired of seeing someone else wearing the "Bling?" Diamonds are a girls best friend, but who cares about anyone else when that fabulous stone could be around your finger or neck?
**Includes Simple Money Spells DVD— $21.95**

Author And Practitioner
Maria D' Andrea

**( ) YOUR PERSONAL MEGA POWER SPELLS
Includes Free 60 Minute DVD – "Put A Spell
On You 'Cause Your Mine!"**

Hundreds of spells that are so powerful their practitioners were once put to death for being witches. Includes spells for protection against unseen forces. Spells for love and romance. Spells for drawing the cornucopia of luck into your life. Spells for creating positive cash flow to enhance your prosperity. Spells for a healthy life. Spells for divining life's purposes with positive magick. Spells for faxing your heart's desires through meditation and visualization. — **$24.00**

**EXPLORE THE SPIRITUAL WORLD
WITH MARIA - MINI WORKSHOPS
AND SEMINARS NOW ON DVD**

Check Off Desired Titles: $10 each
– 3 for $22.00  10 for $79.95
All 16 just $99.95

1. ( ) **Rearrange Your Life With Positive Energy**
2. ( ) **Adventures Of A UFO Tracker With Tim Beckley And Maria**
3. ( ) **The Amazing Power Of Tesla Energy**
4. ( ) **2012 And Beyond – What Can We Expect?**
5. ( ) **Manifesting A New Reality**
6. ( ) **Exploring The Healer Within You**
7. ( ) **Spiritual And Magickal Runes**
8. ( ) **Soul Mind Dreaming**
9. ( ) **Gemstones How They Rock**
10.( ) **Tap To Manifest**
11.( ) **Angels And The Fall**
12.( ) **A Shamanic Life**
13.( ) **Surrender – Effortless Techniques**
14.( ) **The Power Of Planting Positive Seeds**
15.( ) **Attracting A Relationship**
16.( ) **Gemstones And Your Chakras**

Ordering Information: Each Episode Of Exploring The Spiritual World Of Maria is approximately 30 minutes in length and are of broadcast quality. Add $5.00 for S/H.

*(Because of their low price these DVDs are shipped in sleeves. Cases not included).*

**( ) OCCULT GRIMOIRE
AND MAGICAL FORMULARY**

Cover Art by Carol Ann Rodriguez

Ten books in one! – Over 500 spells! Over 200 oversized pages! With the help of this book you will learn: To manifest your own future destiny. To prevent psychic attack. To use herbal magnets. To apply candle magic to receive individual blessings. To unlock secrets of love potions. To mix the best mystical incense. To draw on the powers of crystals and stones. How prayer really works. The only true application for ritualistic oils. — **$25.00**

**( ) SPECIAL OFFER OF THESE 3 BOOKS/DVDS BY
MARIA — $59.95 + $8 P/H**

ORDER DIRECTLY FROM:
TIMOTHY G. BECKLEY, BOX 753
NEW BRUNSWICK, NJ 08903

www.ingramcontent.com/pod-product-compliance
Lightning Source LLC
Chambersburg PA
CBHW080508110426
42742CB00017B/3033